Lobster

the kosher way

Garbo Garbo

An environmentally friendly book printed and bound in England by
www.printondemand-worldwide.com

Mixed Sources
Product group from well-managed
forests, and other controlled sources
www.fsc.org Cert no. TT-COC-002641
© 1996 Forest Stewardship Council

FSC

PEFC

PEFC/16-33-415

PEFC Certified
This product is
from sustainably
managed forests
and controlled
sources
www.pefc.org

This book is made entirely of chain-of-custody materials

www.fast-print.net/store.php

LOBSTER THE KOSHER WAY
Copyright © Garbo Garbo 2014

A catalogue record for this book is available from the British Library

ISBN 978-178456-082-9

First published 2014 by
FASTPRINT PUBLISHING
Peterborough, England.

ONE

My earliest recollection, probably at about the age of three, is of the contents of a bottle of milk being poured over my head by a practical joke loving milkman. Unfortunately for me he lived next door to the fish and chip shop owned by my parents in a working class area of Cardiff in South Wales.

My father, who always considered himself a bit of an entrepreneur, left my mother when he was 40 to live with his mistress and at the age of 60 died of too much whisky. His mistress obviously loved him so much that three weeks after his death she took an overdose of something that did the trick and killed her. Obviously she didn't think much of life without "her man".

My mother was always a strange woman throughout her life, well into old age. At over eighty she could be seen riding my old, battered bike, dressed in layers of my old, out of date and out of shape clothes that I hadn't worn since my teens, many years before. She would often wear two or three hats, one on top of the other, to protect her from the elements and anything else that could befall and old and wobbly cyclist on the busy downtown roads of Cardiff. She rejoiced in being known as the "eccentric millionaire".

My relationship with my mother was terrible for many years, but now I am older I do not hurt from her any more and she is far less "a thing" in my life these days.

Both my father and I hated her. As I grew up (or was trying to) she always said I was ugly, which was not something I needed at that difficult time. Or any time for that matter. It wasn't until years later that I'd like to think, by candlelight, that I was "almost beautiful". I like to think that I have come to terms with the fact that I'm OK. That I'm attractive.

My father had more faith in me and made sure I had something "to stand me in good stead", as he used to say, by seeing to it that I attended the School for Drama in Cardiff Castle, a cold relic left by the Normans after some battle of occupation. It was in this world of words and drama, in the cold, high ceilinged rooms of the Castle, that I was able to lose myself and forget the house I shared with bitter parents. The house that lacked love, caring, warmth, understanding and all the things a real home should have. I came to realize years later that a loving home is not an entitlement, that life has its passages to ride through. But back then I suffered and so lived by acting. So much so that my earlier life became one big act and whilst it is hard to relinquish the protection of "an act" it is only when one is completely whole and at ease with things – and life – that it can be done.

I can remember being five and my father taking me to visit his parents who lived a couple of hours away in the valley town of Brynmawr, not far from the Brecon Beacons. When we returned home my mother and Aggie, our maid, were both out and my father needed to go out. Even though I cried and begged him to stay with me until Aggie or my mother came home he wouldn't and left me alone in the house. Being daylight he didn't think to switch a light on before he left and as the hours passed so did the light. I was too small to reach the light switch and when my mother did eventually come home she found me sitting at the top of the stairs sobbing and terrified of the dark and from the many hours alone in a frightening place.

I don't think I was a particularly good child but in my own defence, it was a childhood during which I was very neglected. Winter and summer my mother would put me to bed at 5 o'clock so that she would be free to open up the fish shop and as I couldn't tell the time she would tell me it was 7 o'clock which was my "bedtime". When I eventually found out my mother had tricked me and lied to me so consistently I was extremely upset.

During one summer when I was supposed to be in bed I would often creep downstairs, out through the side door and, still in my nightie, push my doll's pram all the way to the Cowbridge public house, about four miles along the main arterial road. Unfortunately, after quite a few of these illicit adventures, I was recognised by one of the fish and chip shop customers who hauled me home and "shopped" me. I can't remember exactly how old I was at the time , probably three or four I think, but I do remember that I must have been an excellent curser because I swore violently all the way. On my arrival my surprised and unsuspecting mother got my father to give me a good hiding. After that I was locked in my bedroom at night so no more outings for me.

I was born just a little before the second world war and once it started it seemed to me that virtually every night was spent on a bunk in a beehive shaped, damp, cold corrugated tin air raid shelter called a "Morrison". One incident I recall quite vividly was being four and spending one night at my grandma's, my mother's mother, house in Cardiff. I was having a terrible nightmare, in which men were standing over me and peeing on me, when my uncle was called in to fix the "blackout" so we could have the light on without the Germans seeing it and using us as a landmark. I then went back to sleep but unfortunately the nightmare resumed, only this time in bright orange. This only seemed to make it more terrible and ashamed making.

The next morning I went home and that night my Grandma's house was bombed during one of the biggest blitzes on Cardiff. Grandma never used her "Morrison" shelter so it was fortunate that I had not stayed an extra night as the bedroom I had slept in was a pile of unrecognisable rubble and I would have been killed. Luckily for Grandma when the bomb hit she was in the kitchen baking bread for the Sabbath and the kitchen was completely unscathed. Just goes to show when your numbers up, it's up and when it isn't, it isn't!

I was a lonely, only child but I had a vivid imagination to compensate and my teddy bears and dolls were the brothers and sisters I never had. I could play school with them and make them do just what was needed. I also remember my good luck when I actually stole a real life baby to play with. Its mother had parked her large, comfortable pram outside the fish shop while she bought her chips for lunch so I just wheeled it round to the back of the shop, behind the shelter, where the baby slept out of view. No one knew where it was and the mother was frantic but as I was desperate for a baby brother or sister I just thought this was an easy way to get one. When the pram was discovered the mother was understandably relieved to get her baby back but I remember just being very upset at losing it. Luckily I was considered too young at five for anything to happen to me by way of retribution.

As the war years continued my time was taken up with school, drama classes , perpetual air raids and the fear of the "Jerries" (as I knew the adults called the German bombers) dropping their bombs on my country and my childhood. I also remember I had to carry a Mickey Mouse gas mask with me wherever I went (in case of a "Gas Attack", whatever that was). Fortunately I only ever had to wear it for practices.

The days were difficult, especially having to deal with lessons after so many disturbed and disrupted nights. I don't think I ever got used to that. I was always frightened of the bombings, particularly when, after a bad attack, I went out into my once familiar street and could only see piles of unrecognisable rubble and spaces where the houses once were. And there was also the inevitable "Morrison" shelter with its cold and damp and the inevitable slugs, snails and big black spiders.

Food was generally very short as well although I was probably lucky inasmuch I grew up on good old fish and chips. Even now, after all these years when I get back to England after being away that's the first thing I want.

One "foody" thing that I remember happened when I was 10, about a year after the war ended. My mother had been bedridden for quite a while with sciatica and, in an attempt to help out, I was making gallant, but not terribly successful, attempts to do the cooking. So much so that when a friend of my mother's came to see how she was getting on, my mother asked her if she could make us an omelette. At the time we only had particularly awful dried, substitute eggs (like most people) – nothing like eggs at all really. Paula, the friend, said she was "wizard" with these eggs, "plenty of practice, dear" and off she went, returning shortly proudly bearing her plates of "omelettes". My mother and I tucked in with relish, but then looked at each other. The "omelettes" were absolutely horrible with all the flavour and consistency of cardboard, but we had no alternative but to pretend to eat them. Paula, luckily needed the "Loo" and while she was out of the room we quickly scraped the congealed cardboard "stuff" onto a newspaper and popped it under the bed. I couldn't stop my giggles, even when my mother gave me one of her "looks". Paula, on her return, seeing the empty plate, said "Oh, you did enjoy my cooking. I told you I was a wizard with eggs. Would you like some more?" We declined.

Although food was still rationed and in short supply during the immediate post war years, shops were able to stay open late and, because my mother suffered so much with her sciatica, my father made me work in the shop until it closed at midnight.

No more in bed at 5 o'clock for me then.

TWO

It was an unusually hot summer and I felt I would collapse from fatigue. I worked in the shop seven days a week, seven nights a week for six weeks with no break and no time off. I remember a summer fair on the waste ground opposite the shop and every time I hear the tune "Home in Pasadena" I am ten years old again, in the shop, in the heat and desperately wanting to run free to ride the swing chairs. To blow the smell of hot oil frying (the smell of my childhood) out of my nose and out of my senses. I don't think I ever did make it to the fair.

I can also remember the taste of Tizer (popular before Coke came on the scene) which somehow quenched your thirst quickly but immediately after seemed to leave you more thirsty than before. I believe such sweet drinks are given to Israeli soldiers serving in the desert as it makes them drink more fluids.

But the over riding memory is of the smell of fish and chips and the never ending line of customers waiting to be served by an increasingly work weary me.

There was a period when we moved around a lot and we lived for a time in a flat and then moved again to a newly built house. My father even tried his hand at something new and bought a sweet shop. It meant that whilst I still worked as hard as ever at least I was selling something different in ice creams and sweets. I remember sweets were still rationed then and customers had coupons and ration books and I hope I didn't cheat too many of them through my ignorance of the system. With all this work in the shop I didn't get too much time to enjoy the new house, or even feel any familiarity with it. Just as well really since it wasn't long before my father sold it and we moved yet again to a really dilapidated and slummy fish and chip shop in one of the worst working class area in Cardiff.

Throughout these changes and moves my mother and father continued to quarrel all the time. I never really got used to the continual shouting between them, it was so frightening. My father would often leave the house on these all too frequent occasion, returning home in the small hours, when the fighting and screaming would invariably start all over again.

After years of these bitter quarrels, which seemed to me to get more and more violent, I came home from school one day to find my mother sitting and sobbing in the kitchen. "Your fathers gone off with his coover (Yiddish for prostitute). He's gone because you're such an ugly bitch"

It was from the slummy fish and chip shop he walked out on us, leaving my mother and me together in almost uninhabitable living conditions. The loo was in the yard. Taking a bath meant boiling water downstairs and then carrying it in buckets up the stairs to fill a rusty old bath. The kitchen was often overrun with cockroaches and everything still smelled of stale oil. I always felt sick at home and hated having to sleep in the same bed as my mother, particularly as the only pair of sheets we had for the bed were hardly ever changed. I did try to wash them once but with no hot water and no proper conveniences it was virtually impossible. After this attempt my mother was furious and insulted my feeble efforts "A lady you've become all of a sudden-clean sheets she wants"

During this time I was invariably shabbily dressed in garments that always could do with a good wash. As a result I always felt that other people looked down on me. And although this effected my school work I still had my drama lessons which raised my spirits, and put me above my mother's level of thoughts. More often than not I was chosen to play the lead in the annual school plays and, more importantly, at the drama school as well. But underlying it all was my deep feeling of inferiority that my home life and my dirty clothes caused. It has taken many years and many challenges to overcome this feeling and today I think I have the opposite – not so good either I think.

I wasn't a popular girl and felt I was always on the outside looking in, never being a part of things or belonging. I didn't want to be with the girls who dressed like me, for some reason I thought of them as "poor scruffy things with no homes" and never associated my predicament with them. I think I always thought we were rich in money and therefore different.

On the other hand I was too embarrassed to try and join in with the kids I felt I could relate to because I felt as far as they were concerned I was one of the poor scruffy ones. I just couldn't win. I also felt that after my father had left us everyone knew about it and was laughing at me. Divorce then, in the forties, was something to be ashamed of.

My self image was not helped by how I felt I looked then. I would study my face in the mirror and see a pale, thin face with black eyes and long straight hair. I started to believe my mother – I really was an ugly bitch. I was so ashamed, I just didn't know what to do to improve or alter my looks. I hit on the idea that maybe talcum powder would do the trick. It didn't, of course, and only made me look as if I was going to die in the not too distant future. I wouldn't be surprised if naivety is a staple condition for most fourteen year olds. It certainly was for me.

It was round about this time that my mother decided to look for my father and after much searching discovered he was living in Manchester with his woman. My mother was determined to go and find the "hideout", as she called it, that he shared with his "coover". She also felt she should take me with her as moral support and to put emotional pressure on my father "to come back to us".

To help make the "winning back of husband" occasion my mother went on an extensive shopping spree to glam herself up. I, as you can imagine, was left in my scruffy, unwholesome state.

The eventful day for the "visit" came and we travelled to Manchester. I will never forget the way my heart banged inside me as I climbed the stairs behind my mother in the block of flats where my father lived. We came to the door of my unsuspecting father and his mistress and knocked. He opened the door, saw us standing there, and his face turned grey. I was choked and swallowed, blinded by my tears.

My mother made a terrible scene and I couldn't believe the obscenities she bellowed out. My father was a refined man and, although I didn't want to admit it, his woman looked like a decent sort of lady. But I hated her, she had stolen my father. I stood there and looked at her and asked myself that if my father wanted to live with her and not me what was I worth. My answer was not much.

We went into the flat and I remember crying a lot and asking him to come home with us. After much arguing too and fro he took us to a kosher restaurant in the ghetto area of Manchester to talk. He said he loved "his lady" but he loved me as well and that I would understand it all one day, when I was older, and in the mean time I was to live with my mother. No arrangements were made to see him again and as far as he was concerned that was that.

We stayed at a boarding house in Manchester for a few days in order that my mother could visit the flat each day to shout abuse at my father and his "lady love" through their door.

Whilst she did so it was completely overlooked that I needed feeding, notwithstanding being heartbroken. I had no money of my own and when I told my mother how hungry I was she called me a nagger and told me to "shut your mouth". The daughter of the landlady where we were staying was round about my age and we became friendly. She felt sorry for the situation I was in, realized how hungry I was and smuggled soup to me from the kitchen. I had to eat it far from the gaze of the landlady who was busy serving meals to the guests who had actually paid for them.

At the end of the week we returned to Cardiff and for me an even harder and more difficult time with my mother and her unfortunate personality.

THREE

I was fourteen. Time to leave school. Even though my mother had plenty of money she had no intention of spending any on me and any form of further education, particularly if I could work and pay my way. I still attended to drama school at night as no fee was needed because I had a scholarship. I so desperately wanted to be an actress and attend drama school full time but the pressure my mother put on me to earn a wage was intolerable.

My mother found a hairdressing apprenticeship for me, where she didn't have to pay the normal apprenticeship fee, so that was that. I absolutely hated it. I could never make hair do the things it was supposed to do and I disliked intensely the close contact with the women. To make things even more horrible the woman I worked for was very smart, very bossy and very, very intimidating. She also continually told me that I smelt of chips. Well she was right about that. The trouble was that the smell was attached to the only coat I had, an old raincoat I had to wear to keep me warm as I cycled to work. To this day I have never owned another raincoat.

My mother "hijacked" all my earnings to pay for the few meals I ate at home and even ransacked my purse and helped herself to cash I may have earned from tips. I had seen her do it on more than one occasion but when I confronted her she just swore at me and said she was "insulted". Later though my mother's sister, Janey, told me that my mother would boast to her that she had taken the money and even laughed at how she had denied it in response of my accusations. Janey said that my mother was a strange and difficult women and she couldn't see how she was part of the same family.

About the only good thing that came out of my apprenticeship was the fact that the salon in which I worked was in the basement of a five star hotel and I could therefore eat, at the very good discounted price of one shilling, in their elegant dining room. The benefit of doing so was twofold. I could eat good food at a good price but at the same time it gave me a glimpse of a lifestyle that would take me away from the one I was used to.

The Hotel was always full of famous people and in the dining room I contrived to have interesting conversations with many of them, including Jean Simmons; Richard Burton; Danny Kaye; Moira Shearer; Beniamino Gigli and many others. These stars often ate alone and it only seemed natural to me to smile at them, even to start a conversation. It was a different world I was learning about and I knew it was important for me to develop a certain style of my own.

My Aunt Janey lent me money to buy clothes with the understanding that I would pay her back so much each week. I am pleased to say I never missed on our agreement. She helped and encouraged me, she installed values in me which have stayed with me my whole life. She, unlike my mother, didn't swear or curse and, most importantly, I loved her dearly and this was returned. She was my first true friend and confidante and played the major role in helping me through a difficult adolescence. I recall going to her after one particularly upsetting incident that occurred in my teen years and the help she gave.

I was kissing a particular young man goodnight when I thought, for some unknown reason that I cannot for the life of me think of now, I heard his shoelaces rustling. Looking down to see why he was so interested in his feet I quickly realised that it was quiet a different part of his anatomy when I saw his fly was open and he was drawing a condom over his large, quivering, hard penis. Shocked, I screamed and quickly left, happy in the knowledge that the hardest thing now was the slap I gave him before I rushed away. Sex had entered my life and had left me shaking, unfortunately not with desire but a sense of disquiet and grubbiness.

I took a taxi and went straight to see Aunt Janey. Apart from periods I knew nothing about the facts of life but I knew Janey would be able to help. And she did. She was able to enlighten me and explain things in such a way that made me feel clean again. The funny thing is that because Janey had one eye much smaller than the other she always felt freaky and kept her distance from men, therefore remaining a virgin all her life. But that night she was wonderful and helped me immensely. I always thought she was fascinating and was devastated when she died of cancer when she was only 40 years old.

But back to my perennial problem. My mother. By the time of my mid to late teens my mother had started another business, credit drapery - a sort of old fashioned catalogue way of shopping. I bought many of my clothes from her for which, I learned later, I paid highly inflated prices. And to add insult to injury she would more often than not wear them whilst I was at work. She was fat and none too clean so my clothes would invariably become out of shape and rather smelly. When I accused her of "borrowing" my clothes she would resort to her standard tactics and swear loud and long and call me a "lying bitch".

18

As I approached my 17th birthday I was determined to have a special party to celebrate, but certainly not at home. By now I was living in two completely different worlds. The glamorous, exciting one at the hotel and the sordid, grubby one at home.

I definitely knew which one I preferred.

I decided that the party would be held at the country club, mainly because it had a certain panache that I liked but also because it was in a beautiful setting in a delightfully named place called St Melons just outside Cardiff.

The party was a great success and a wonderful evening. Frog legs sautéed in butter and garlic, delicately poached fresh salmon, pheasant stuffed with prunes, a tossed green salad all to be followed by strawberries, cigars, brandy and coffee. The food was all of the highest quality and the cigars and brandy on offer were the best possible. All a far cry from my mother's filthy kitchen which, more than once, managed to produce the odd fried cockroach as an accompaniment to her other dire offerings. I didn't tell my mother about the party. I wanted it to be mine and unspoilt.

That party, that evening, certainly set the style and the pattern for the rest of my life.

Although I say it myself it was around that time that I decided that I was an attractive girl and I started to date a man named Joe, who was twenty five. I thought it was going well, we seemed to be getting on and enjoying each others company, when one evening whilst we were out for a drive, he stopped the car, put his head on the steering wheel and told me his parents had arranged a marriage for him. I was stunned. He had said so many times that he loved me and, although still only seventeen, I thought we would be married when I was a little older. It transpired that his parents had approached my mother regarding a dowry but she had given them short shrift and sent them packing saying I would not get a penny of her "hard earned gelt". A Dowry, in those days, was not unusual in the Jewish tradition to which I belonged. His parents had then searched for someone who they felt was more "suitable" for their son and found him a wife – who just happened to take seventy nine thousand pound to the marriage. So much for love.

I was eighteen, I had just finished my nine month happy, but innocent, relationship with Joe and was feeling very low, when I saw my father again. I hadn't seen him for many years and on a hot, humid day in June when I was out walking aimlessly in the City my father walked past. It took my breath away but I was devastated when he didn't recognize me. My sadness was compounded and I became even more sad and lonely, my faith in relationships at rock bottom. I definitely thought that phones only rang for other people.

In the August, after two months of despair something happened that would change my life.

My mother had taken it upon herself to arrange for me to visit a woman she knew vaguely in order to cut her hair. I really didn't want to do it. I had been working until ten o'clock most nights during the week and to late afternoon most Saturdays for quite a while and was tired. I really didn't need the extra work and certainly wasn't relishing the prospect. I complained to my mother but, as usual, my words fell on deaf ears.

Had I known beforehand what was to result from that visit, on a hot Sunday afternoon, to a fat lady to cut her hair I most certainly wouldn't have gone.

But I did and the rest, as they say, is history.

FOUR

It was in a bedroom in a sort of slum flat belonging to the fat woman that I met Ivan Jacob Levinson. He was twenty five, short, thickset, with a blond, thick wavy head of hair, large grey slightly protruding eyes, a straight nose and a wonderful smile that lit up his face completely. Only later in our relationship did I discover he also had a chip on his shoulder far bigger than any I had ever served.

He was a pharmacist, managing the Co-Op pharmacy in the valley town of Mountain Ash where he had lodgings. His mother had died of a massive heart attack about six years prior to me meeting him. His father, not wishing to be alone following her death had proposed to, and been accepted by, the fat woman whose hair I was doing – and who just happened to be his ex wife's sister.

When I met her she and Ivan's father were engaged but the sad, and bizarre, thing is that just before they were to be married she dropped dead of the same thing, in the same spot, as her sister. Even more bizarrely, Ivan's father then married yet a third sister. She turned out to be the stepmother from hell, a very nasty piece of work. Carrying on the family trait she also died suddenly and fairly young, this time from a burst appendix.

After graduating Ivan had wanted to stay on to study medicine but as his parents had no money his time to study came to an end and he became a pharmacist.

He asked me out, I was flattered and we started dating. He was generous and kind and, like me, had no real home life which somehow made it all the more important to us. After about three weeks of going out together Ivan asked me to marry him and I agreed. Not, as it turned out, one of my better decisions.

I was 19 when we married and I remember my "special day" for all the wrong reasons. The wedding left a lot to be desired. My mother financed the "affair" and I can remember my guests having to toast the Bride & Groom with empty glasses. The guests had also been told by my mother to give cash presents – "Give gelt" I think was her request – and these collectively managed to pay for our miserable honeymoon in the Channel Islands.

When we married we were both still virgins and even remained so for the first few months of the marriage. Not for Ivan's want of trying. It seemed to me that he had a large sexual appetite and wanted to make love to me and touch me all the time. Eventually I succumbed, and immediately became pregnant. I missed nine periods, just not believing what was happening to me. And then the realization dawned. I felt sick nearly all the time, so sick that everything tasted of poison. The swelling tummy got bigger and bigger, as did my craving for pickles. All I felt, all the time, was fat, tired and sick.

Gradually I also came to loathe the act and stickiness of sex, a feeling not helped by the fact that his body induced a feeling of nausea in me.

Whilst he loved me obsessively I quickly understood he also had the capacity to be cruel, possessive and quarrelsome. It wasn't long before I started to dislike not only his personality and attitudes, but also his looks. I became very disillusioned and disappointed with my marriage. He had told me he that he loved the "arts" but I never saw him read a book or listen to the music he professed to love and know so much about. All he seemed to care about was his health and all he seemed to want to do was quarrel with people, particularly his many employers. He was a great complainer.

It became evident to me fairly quickly in our life together that he was a "lightweight" with a lot of problems with himself, none more so than a destructive personality.

The nine months of pregnancy were to me, sheer purgatory, but eventually the day to give birth came, albeit almost two weeks late, and after a long, painful and natural childbirth a boy, later to be called Ashley, was born.

Ivan was rude and impatient with the hospital staff and even quarrelled, very loudly, with my mother in a ward full of new mothers. All of which upset me terribly. After the usual ten days in hospital it was time to go home but Ivan did not pick us up, a neighbour did. On the same day he arrived home at six o'clock and demanded that in future his meals should always be ready, and the baby in bed, when he got home. And that was the way it was after that. He never had to wait for a meal or have the baby around him at mealtimes.

The strange thing was that Ivan was proud of his first born and loved him dearly. I would breast feed the baby but then he would insist on supplementing the feeding. The problem with this overindulgence was that the baby became fat and unhealthy and later had to be operated on to cure a fatty hernia.

No such thing as "the pill" then but because I hated sex so much I refused to wear a diaphragm and about nine months after Ashley was born, to my horror and disbelief, I was pregnant. Again I had to endure the traumas, the fatness, the tiredness, the sickness of pregnancy. And then Sara was born.

At the time of the birth Ivan was working for a private company as a pharmacy manager, and we had moved. Yet again he hated his employer but things weren't too bad.

I found it very boring having to look after two young babies but when Sara was thirteen months we left Cardiff and moved to Cheshunt in Hertfordshire when Ivan got a new job, and again worked for the Co-Op as manager. We lived in a small flat next to his shop. It was no surprise to me when Ivan very quickly started to complain and hate his employer.

About a year after we moved our third child was conceived. Again the pregnancy was not an enjoyable time, but this time it was compounded by the fact that Ivan was portraying very strange, odd behaviour. Six weeks before the baby was due he told me that the doctor, after a routine examination of the baby, had informed him that only a head and body could be felt but no limbs. I was terrified throughout the remainder of the pregnancy that I was about to give birth to a monster!

When I went into labour Ivan refused to give me gas and air and even refused to stay with me. I can remember quite clearly holding on to his tie to try and keep him with me but he pushed my hand aside and left. For whatever the reasons I knew I was alone and could not rely on him for any kind of support. I knew he was a weak and frightened man. From the beginning of my labour and through the dry, long birth he was no help whatsoever, and I hated him.

The midwife needed gas and air for me but because Ivan had refused to get it she couldn't help me. My body seemed to be breaking in two. I asked God to let me die. But I heard Sara singing Humpty Dumpty in the next room and her voice bought me back and I knew I mustn't die. I just hoped my baby would be as good and easy as my little blond singing girl.

At six in the morning my son was born – with all his bits.

I was twenty four years old but looked and felt a lot older for quite a while.

THREE PREGNANCIES

The woman was nineteen, a virgin and ugly. The man was twenty five, also a virgin. The wedding was unusual only because the guests toasted with empty glasses. The honeymoon was over. The woman missed nine periods. At first unbelieving, then sick, then swelling, then a desire for pickles, then fat and tired.

She liked the names Jezebal and Bathsheba. She got bigger and bigger and eventually the time came to give birth. It was late – eleven days, each day an eternity.

She awoke with pains and a neighbour took her to the hospital. The man had gone to work. At the hospital she was prepared. Shaved, examined, enemaed and left. All day without a drink. She had more pains and was made to get up and walk. The pain was unbearable and she was sick.

The man arrived at six in the evening and demanded a sleeping draft for her. She slept and then woke to find herself bearing down so was wheeled to the delivery room. She worked hard through the pain and at 10.15 she felt a wet slither between her legs and saw a blue boy with puffy eyes. He looked ugly. She wanted to phone the man and ask for fish and chips.

The child was difficult, the woman was young. The relationship was bad. He was too demanding. The woman loved him but tried not to love him too much in case she lost him. She didn't think she could cope with that. She tried to make herself invulnerable to him. She succeeded but the child felt it and that wasn't good. The child was very fat. Lethargic and bored. The man loved him and gave him a lot of attention. The boy was late to walk, late to talk. He was a difficult boy.

27

When the boy was nine months old the woman was pregnant again. She was unbelieving, sick, impatient, fat, tired and resigned. The boy was put with the woman's mother before the birth. It was a mistake. The boy was depressed. Fat. Lethargic.

The new baby was late and the woman waited. She was anxious. She took castor oil with orange juice. She finally saw a show of blood. She laboured all night and in the morning went to the hospital. She was made to walk around until four in the afternoon. The doctor told her she had been wrong to take castor oil. At six o'clock she was taken to the delivery room and at six fifteen she had a ginger girl. The woman wanted eggs, toast and tea.

The relationship between the woman and the girl was very strong. The woman loved her and was not nervous. The girl was a fat, blond placid baby with round eyes. She and the boy became close and she did a lot for him. He broke her toys. The woman would punish him always.

The girl was three, with close cropped hair. She stood in the sun in the garden. One strap of her homemade dress slipped off her shoulder. The girl was totally engrossed in the butterfly she had captured, with all it's colours. It was cupped in her small hands. She was unaware of eyes observing her. The girl sniffed as if taking in the smell and texture of her captive. Her blond head lifted a moment, she seemed deep in thought. She looked back at the butterfly and then, in a flash, pulled its wings apart and ate them. She then skipped away humming softly, running free.

Two years after the girl was born the woman was pregnant again. Again she was horrified, fat and sick. The

28

boy and the girl were very caring for the woman. Six weeks before the birth the man told the woman that a doctor had told him that the bay had no limbs. The man said that it was probably just a trunk. The woman was horrified and had nightmares.

In due course the woman's waters broke and the birth began. The man was asked to fetch gas and air. He refused. During the birth the woman took hold of the man's tie and asked him to stay with her. He wrenched the tie away and left her alone. The woman, in her pain had visions of fire . She knew she could never trust or rely on the man again. Whatever happened she knew she was alone. She hated him.

The child, a boy, was born, complete, and wrapped in a caul. She felt this child to be completely hers.

FIVE

Ivan became stranger and stranger. He lost his job, but luckily I had persuaded him to buy a house, so at least we hadn't lost our home with the job.

A neighbour, Mrs Elsley, played a major part in our lives at this time. She could see how things were in our house and was very sorry for our predicament. She loved the children, was very fond of me, and offered lots of helpful advice. She really did become a mother figure to us all. She suggested that I talk to a friend of ours, who was a consultant at the Westminster Hospital, about Ivan.

I took Mrs Elsey's advice and told the consultant of Ivan's cyclic behaviour and his inability to cope, how he complained about each new job (there seemed an awful lot) and how bad things were. He seemed incoherent most of the time. His hands wouldn't coordinate, his food would slip off his fork on to his clothes. He foamed at the mouth, wet the bed, shat on the stairs, took nocturnal walks and got lost. On one occasion he lost his salary, on another bought home thirteen ponds of kosher sausages and two large salami. The bills and the mortgage were unpaid.

I hated him more and more. The children and I were afraid of his terrible, moody behaviour. I never knew how, when he was in work, he managed to fill the prescriptions. After losing one job his employer told me he thought Ivan was quite mad.

I knew Ivan was prescribed tablets for his high blood pressure and I knew he couldn't stop taking them. He was the same with many of the other pills that didn't suit him but he never sought any proper treatment or diagnosis.

The children and I put up with a lot of mental cruelty and I eventually came to the conclusion that I would leave him. I consulted a lawyer and she agreed, in view of everything I told her, that I had grounds for divorce. When Ivan received the petition he became even more strange and mad. He painted a picture of Sara in which she was completely scarlet. He threatened to kill me and brandished a knife at my throat. He even locked us out of the house and threatened to burn it down whilst he was still inside. We were terrified as we stood outside. It seemed to be very quiet for a long time so we broke in to see what was happening. We found Ivan in the kitchen with his head in the gas oven, but fortunately, and typical of him, it wasn't on. He was foaming at the mouth and his eyes were bulging.

I put his ever worsening behaviour down to the fact that he was taking such a mixture of pills. In my mind I considered his problem self inflicted which made me both sad and mad. I told him that I wanted him to stop taking the pills and seek proper medical advice and if he did I would stay with him and help. I pleaded with him to try hard as I was at the end of my strength and could no longer cope with him as he was.

He cried a lot and agreed to see a psychiatrist. In the same week he even found a new job where he would be put in a very nice hotel during the week and come home at weekends. The children and I thought this would give us some peace and respite from him but he was phoning a number of times every night, crying for me to go to him. After one such call I agreed to go drive to see him. The problem was that I was a bad, new driver and had difficulty seeing in the dark. This was compounded by the fact it was

31

terribly foggy and as a result I got lost several times. I remember I had to do a "U" turn on a motorway at one stage to avoid, so I thought, being lost, forever stuck on a motorway!

When I did eventually arrive Ivan was incoherent, his eyes glazed. He seemed drugged. He was a pathetic figure but seemed both frightened, and frightening, at the same time. I hated him.

Ashley was eleven, Sara ten and Martin seven when all this was happening and I was increasingly worried and frustrated by what was going on with Ivan. I appealed to friends to talk to him but the problem was that in front of others Ivan appeared rational and normal. I was trapped in a situation of which only I, the children, and our good neighbour Mrs Elsley were aware.

One day when at the home of a friend who was a consultant I told him of Ivan's erratic behaviour and his inability to cope, and my concern about the tablets he was taking continually. I explained the fear under which the children and I were living and Ivan's ability to appear lucid to others whilst frightening to us. Although I begged the friend to help professionally, he was rather reluctant to interfere. He did, however, agree to see us as often as he could over the next couple of months and observe Ivan closely. After doing so he told me he was concerned about Ivan's puffed and swollen ankles and that he should go to the Westminster Hospital for a check up. When he told Ivan the same thing because he thought he might have a heart problem Ivan sat, transfixed in a chair for what seemed days, until at last he was admitted to hospital.

At the hospital Ivan went into a fit which the doctors initially thought was epileptic but later realized it was the effect of his withdrawal from the many drugs he had been taking to keep himself going. When I visited him he professed not to know who I was but when some friends turned up five minutes later he recognised them without a moments hesitation. I was convinced that Ivan was self destructive and had a self induced illness but I was hopeful that treatment and therapy could cure him. I visited him every day he was in the hospital.

Ivan had lost yet another job and so I took a part time job in a store, working at the perfume counter. It helped a little but after paying for petrol to get to work and buying fruit for Ivan there was virtually nothing left to pay bills or for food. I knew nothing of social security so for the next few weeks the children and I ate virtually nothing but jacket potatoes with grated cheese and drank only milk. The reasons for such an unvarying diet, whilst primarilly financial also had two other reasons. One, I was beyond thinking about changing diets and secondly, ironically, down to Ivan. In one of his "eccentric" moments before going into hospital he had purchased, as if for a small army rather than a family of five, three huge bags of potatoes. So I had the readymade basis of a nutritious and inexpensive, albeit repetitive, meal. To this day none of the family can see a jacket potato without conjuring up memories of that time.

On one occasion, during our "potato" period, we were invited out to dinner at a friend's home, after our evening visit to see Ivan in the hospital. The children and I ate great quantities of food, far too quickly, whilst grinning at each other across the table. The sheer pleasure of eating good food was wonderful and gave us all the fortitude to return to our cheese potatoes and milk diet the next day.

During this whole period I don't think any of our friends had any idea as to how poor and hungry we were. All we had was the little – the very little – I made and the unpaid bills just mounted up and up.

After six weeks in the hospital Ivan came home. He was slimmer, coherent and seemed fairly normal. I was still very nervous and still felt I was not going to cope but he said he felt so much better. He said all the trouble had been his high blood pressure which was now controlled, and would continue to be so, by the medication he was on.

He seemed fine and no longer appeared strange, or threatening. In fact he looked, and acted, better than he had for years. He even managed to find another job.

But it was an illusion. The tablets he had to control his blood pressure began to have a strange effect on him and he would, without warning, suddenly fall to the floor with a dreadful thump.

He was still working however and I would take him to and collect him from work each day. One evening when I picked him up and he got into the car he went a most deathly grey. Worst still blood started to spurt from his face. I was terrified and drove like a mad thing to the nearest hospital. He stayed there two days.

It was not long after I collected him and took him home that things started to deteriorate quite dramatically and he reverted to being frightening and threatening. He also started to act even more peculiarly than ever. It was then he wet the bed and shat on the stairs. He looked glazed and spaced out. He became impotent, which I certainly didn't mind! Everything was becoming a nightmare again and I felt that this time trying to deal with him and look after the kids was far too much to deal with.

34

I knew that all the symptoms Ivan was displaying, both the old ones combined with the new ones, were certainly not indicative of improving health and I went to see the doctor friend who had originally placed him in the hospital. I wanted to know what was going on. I also wanted a divorce.

He referred me to the consultant who had been in charge of Ivan's case and about a week later I was called to the hospital to see him. He told me that Ivan had severely damaged kidneys but was unsuitable for dialysis as he was mentally and physically too weak to cope with such treatment. The consultant told me that Ivan, still only thirty nine, had about five years to live.

He also told me to expect Ivan to die in a uremic coma. Six months later he did, dramatically and pathetically.

Ivan was dead at thirty nine and I was a widow at thirty two. I had no money, no family, no profession and three children. The one small consolation was that Ivan, just before he sank into the coma, told me I had been a good wife.

Ivan's funeral was terrible.

His father wheeled the corpse to the burial place, in a sort of box made from orange box wood, apparently for quick deterioration to speed up the entrance into heaven. It looked like some sort of wheelbarrow. Ivan's father was a small man, about five feet tall and the crotch of his trousers came right down to his knees.

The whole scene was macabre, horrible and unreal. So much so that I became hysterical with laughter, and rolled around on the grass.

Things became worse when the coffin was opened for me to say goodbye to Ivan, as I knew he would have wanted. As I looked in it didn't look like his face at all. And as I looked around at his friends' faces they all slowly changed into skulls. It was horrible.

After the funeral I went home, leaving the children with a cousin for the night, drank a bottle of scotch and screamed and screamed. I was a widow and I knew the challenge was there. I knew what I had to do but was a little unclear as to how to do it. What I was sure of was the need for me to have a break.

A CHAPTER CLOSES

The wife met the husband at the station. Eight thirty. It was a warm summer evening. The husband got into the car, the wife kissed him, and the journey home started. Suddenly, without warning, blood gushed from all over the husbands face. He looked very grey and very frightened. The wife drove like a crazy thing to the nearest hospital. Blood was all over the seats and the floor of the car. The husband was in the hospital for two days after which he was allowed home.

Little did either know that it was the beginning of the end of the husband's life.

The start of the beginning of the wife's life.

The husband died soon after in a uremic coma at the age of thirty nine. The wife was thirty two.

The funeral when it came was a disaster. They wheeled the husband out on a barrow made from orange box crates. The wife had the coffin opened to say goodbye. The man inside did not seem to look like her husband. The husband's father was wheeling the barrow. He was a small man. Five feet four. The crotch of his trousers reached to his knees. The wife looked around the synagogue at the guests. All their faces seemed to turn to skulls as she looked. The wife started to laugh uncontrollably. She couldn't stop. She laughed more and more, as though possessed.

After the funeral the wife went home alone. She took a bottle of scotch to the marital bed. Although it was no longer the marital bed. She drank the whisky. She screamed and wept. Louder and louder. More and more. She became hysterical. She emptied herself of emotion, and the bottle of whisky.

And then the wife slept.

She awoke much later and began her struggle for survival.

SIX

I was, by this time, an exotic looking woman. The ugly duckling was no longer visible. I decided that a second language was what I needed. French perhaps. My education had been so scanty, and what there had been I had dreamt away on butterfly wings through the classroom window in the summer days of my youth.

So I arranged to have French lessons. Very quickly I discovered two things. Firstly, perhaps languages were not my thing. Secondly, lively and sociable circles of people were. The people I met were a real bonus and I found that I was able to be at one with them. I learned to dance a Flamingo, love a Mauritian, be mistaken for a beautiful Persian, stay up until two- thirty in the morning, enjoy exotic foods. I also learned that I couldn't learn French.

This was the beginning of the knowledge about myself.

I loved it all, life was so full. I would join in such wonderful activities but would suddenly find self awareness taking over and would watch such scenes from outside of myself. I would wonder what I was doing there, who was I and how had I become part of such a magical place. Was it a kind of freedom, a time for healing and forgetting things? A time for finding my true feelings and discovering the real me.

I realized that this kaleidoscopic way of life was a stepping stone in my life and that I would use it, and enjoy it to the full, until I no longer felt I needed it.

But I'm racing ahead of things.

Just after I became a widow my friends suggested I should have a break. They further suggested I should go and stay at a particular hotel in a sedate little English seaside town. A hotel known for its clientele of widows and elderly people. I agreed with the idea of a break but not with the choice of venue.

I went to Paris.

I did so because I felt I was still searching for something in my life. Although I had no knowledge of French language or currency I knew Paris was the place I needed to visit and I had enough money from a small insurance policy to fulfil the dream. I wanted to refresh my energies. To make myself fit to face the challenges of bringing up my family. To forget the past sick, horrific years. To start again.

I wanted an affair. Enjoyable, exciting sex with a fit, healthy, good looking, virile man. And Paris was the place to find it.

From the moment I walked into the airport lounge in England I felt transformed. I was a traveller, free and ready for life. The hour long flight was a magic carpet ride to a new way of life.

The evening walk along the Seine with the lights reflecting on the water, the smell of coffee, the promising wafts of garlic and spit roasted meats from the Latin Quarter, the atmospheric back streets of the Left Bank are all never to be forgotten memories. I walked until daylight broke bringing a whole new picture of the river. Grey, misty with a certain sordidness with the meth drinking tramps slumped in the arches. I loved, and still love, Paris.

I also found my sexual adventures in Paris.

I met one man and we walked along the Seine and talked for what seemed all night long. Another I met along the boulevard was handsome and intelligent and we had dinner. Neither was "the one".

I then got talking to another in a street café. He was young and handsome and although we had trouble talking, because of the language barrier, we communicated so well in so many other ways.. He took me to Montmartre and the Sacre Coeur and we dined and danced. I took him back to my Pension and we made love. The next day we met again and walked and talked. We ate meats from a wooden platters and again went to my Pension and made love.

On my last day in Paris we met and I ate couscous for the first time. I bought him a beautiful cravat and he made it clear to me that he loved me. He took me to the airport and we promised to meet again in England.

When he phoned me, as agreed, I didn't want to meet him. I had gone to Paris specifically to find something – and him. But, important as he was, he belonged in Paris.

I needed to move on.

SEVEN

I needed a job. I needed a proper income, not just pin money. There were four of us and a mortgage to pay. I was also determined that we should enjoy a high standard of life. But real jobs were difficult to find, particularly for people like me, with no real training or experience. I didn't want social security and was in receipt of a widow's pension of £18 a week. Not much to keep a family on. My mother was no real support, never had been. In fact just before Ivan had died I had asked her to lend me £87 so I could take the whole family, including Ivan, for a holiday. She had point blankly refused, saying "who will pay me back when your husband dies?". She did send me £2 for the first month after Ivan died and then £1 for the second month. After that, nothing.

I discussed the situation with my children. We were, and still are, a very close family. I never told them lies and never hid anything from them. I needed their support, advice, friendship and care. I made it clear to them that I was captain of the ship and didn't need any form of mutiny. I told them of the necessity to get a job and their support. They listened, all sitting round my bed, and agreed that things would not be easy and that they wouldn't make any additional problems. We all agreed that it would make sense for me to look for a job locally because Martin, who was seven, needed me around. It would also save on expensive fares into London.

So I looked though the local paper and soon found an advert for an "Inspector", just round the corner from where we were living. I wasn't sure what an Inspector was – or what was being inspected – but as I had no training in any particular field I felt all fields were open. I was able to get an interview for the job.

The interview was held in a very smart office, and seemed to go well and they seemed to like me. At its end they asked me "Mrs Levinson, are you sure this is really you?" Slightly nonplussed, and still slightly unsure as to what the job was exactly, I replied "But of course. It's what I've always wanted – to be an Inspector. When can I start?"

I was offered the job. No problem, I thought. That evening the children and I celebrated with a glass of sherry.

On my first day Sara brought me breakfast in bed and I gave her instructions to make sure she held Martin's hand all the way to school. I also told Martin to be a good boy. At seven I left for work.

I went to the office, put down my bag, hung up my coat and said to a rather thin man standing nearby "Hello, I'm Mrs Levinson, the new Inspector. Where is my desk? I suppose the girls will bring me all their problems. Maybe you would have a Vogue I could have a look at while I wait"

I was a little disturbed by the difference between the office I was now in and the one in which I had been interviewed. No carpets. No plants. In place of aluminium picture windows there were pokey holes in the wall for ventilation.

The thin man, who told me his name was John, handed me a screwdriver. I said "I don't think so, I don't use screwdrivers". He ignored me and called someone called Mary and told me to sit next to her. I thought she was the first girl to bring me her problems. But oh no! She gave me a thing with a lot of coloured wires coming out of it. She made some reference to them being mixed or unmixed or something and I was supposed to sort them out with the screwdriver! Just then a whistle blew and I was able to stop whatever I was supposed to be doing to the thing with the wires with the screwdriver. Apparently it was time for coffee. This suited me fine, in fact I was going to stop and make a pot of coffee......

I realized that my chair was a lot higher than anyone else's by, what seemed to me, several feet but what nobody told me was that I needed to swivel the chair in one direction to lower it and in another to raise it. I remained in blissful ignorance. I was also told I had to dry the thing with wires with a blower. As I did I managed to blow more air up my skirt than on the thing with wires. When I thought my thing with wires was dry I said to Mary that I had finished. "Oh no, dear" she replied "nobody ever finishes here". She knew. She'd been there twenty years.

That evening when I got home I told Sara not to tell anyone but I wasn't an inspector but a factory girl. I told her about the things with wires and how much trouble I had with them.

After nine days of sheer purgatory I phoned, asked to speak to thin John and told him I had to leave. He said "Mrs Levinson, we loved having you. You were wonderful. You had style. Nobody's had that here before. But I have to say this job is not for you. We'll pay you a month's money even though you only worked nine days. We all had a bet you wouldn't last three. Good Luck, it was nice knowing you"

Over the next few months I seemed to go from one unsuitable job to another. To doing wrong accounts, to putting holiday makers on wrong planes. To managing a felt and hessian shop where I made a deal with my

44

assistant, Linda, that she could come in late when she wanted if she measured all the three quarter pieces of cloth, in all colours and work out the percentages. The owner had a big thing about percentages.

I then had a job in telesales with the largest evening paper in London selling advertising space from which I came home very deaf and very late every night.

One day a job came up over my earphones for a medical rep for a well known and prestigious company which seemed just the thing for me. I feigned a nervous breakdown in order to get the time off to go for the interview.

The interview went well and I was offered the job at one thousand pounds a year, plus a new car. I asked for twelve hundred and we agreed on eleven thousand five hundred. I started the new job by going on a six week intensive training course where I learned about pharmacology and rheumatology and conversed seriously about drugs and their effect and affect. Quite ironic really after a dead husband with a pocketful of pills. Luckily I had some very good friends who had the children whilst I was at the course.

One slight problem at first was the company car. It had five gears and overdrive, whilst my own old banger only had three gears. I therefore often had difficulty in finding the right gear, a problem I solved more often than not by never getting out of second gear.

My area was central London and as we lived twenty five miles out, and traffic was more often than not congested, I usually had to leave about six fifteen each morning to be at my first appointment at eight. My target was to see at least five doctors and three consultants each day and to call six pharmacies and a wholesaler. I had to discuss the benefits of at least four of our products and persuade the GPs to prescribe our drugs. I more often than not would not arrive home in the evening until about eight fifteen, usually with a mountain of paperwork because my days activities had to be recorded on computer cards which had to be posted every night.

What didn't help was my inability to read the London street map, my terrible sense of direction and my limited road sense. In the early days I even kept Sara away from school from time to time to accompany me on my travels. She was an excellent navigator, which made the days go much faster and therefore made them more productive. It was also a lot more fun when she was with me. I had to stop doing this though as she needed to attend school.

The job was hard and I found a nice young French girl as an au pair which helped a lot and eased some of the pressure to keep family and job going. It was, however, still hard going. Suddenly things got tougher when the French girl had to return home because her mother needed her to help run the small family hotel.

I seemed to be living an extremely nocturnal existence, leaving home in the dark very early, getting home in the dark very late. And then starting all over again. I was exhausted.

So exhausted that after six months I had to give up the job and return the lovely car. To compound the change I rented out the house and took the three children and the cat to live in Canada.

EIGHT

I don't know what made me choose Canada, it was pure impulse. But the decision was made. I just knew that I didn't want to stay in England getting up at five thirty every day to make a living while an au pair stayed at home. It just didn't make sense. I wanted a different, and better, way of life. So we all had our vaccinations to travel, all stoically suffering sore arms for a while. It then took me just a week to arrange to rent our house out for a year and our adventure began.

It was a cool day in May when Mrs Elsley cried and kissed us all goodbye, with a special hug for Martin. We all had our specific responsibilities for the journey. Martin was in charge of his duffle bag with the iron, his football and the cat food, Ashley was in charge of the picnic basket in which we had packed our cat Sebastian – a rather fat Siamese and Sara and I had the luggage.

The money for the trip came from the years rent which I'd got in advance for the house. I figured that if we all liked Canada I could get a job, sell the house here in England and buy one over there.

The flight was wonderful, even though Martin managed to drink a little too much free wine because I only became aware of him doing so when it was too late. He had a very red face and shiny eyes. The rest of us were all concerned about the cat, wondering how he was coping in the hold of the plane. When we arrived we found out when he was handed to us, prowling round his turd covered basket, crying as only Siamese cats can. Ashley cleaned him up, Sara gave him a cuddle, we took him for a short walk on his lead and he calmed down, obviously happy to be re-united with the family.

We took a cab to the Sheraton Hotel where I had booked a suite. We were all tired and I particularly wanted to be fresh the following day as I intended to look for an apartment as soon as possible. The rooms in the hotel were lovely and all of us, even Sabby the cat, were comfortable and happy. About five in the evening, as it was still light, I decided we should go out and have a look round and find somewhere to have a bite to eat. Everywhere was so different to the English suburb we had just left. We found somewhere to eat on Yonge Street after which we returned to the hotel, a few blocks away, showered and went to bed.

We awoke a little late the following morning to cries of protest from Sabby who must have thought we had forgotten his breakfast. Once we had fed him we decided we should also eat and visited the hotel's breakfast bar. And what an incredible breakfast bar it was. To us, used to our rather frugal life style in England, there seemed to be so much varied and interesting food. We certainly enjoyed our first breakfast in Canada. Afterwards we walked Sabby, bought a local paper and I started my search for our new home.

We were very lucky in quickly finding a furnished apartment in a good neighbourhood in a block which had a laundry room and a swimming pool! It was also just across a small road from a school which was ideal for Martin, Ashley and Sara. The funny thing is we almost didn't get it. When we arrived to see it we had Sabby in the picnic basket. He wasn't very happy about being confined again and was making quite a lot of noise. The woman caretaker unsure what the strange noise was asked us "You don't have an animal in there do you? Animals are not allowed in this building." With straight faces we all denied having an animal with us. Luckily the woman opened the door to let us in to view the apartment and then left us to it. Our laughter drowned out even more noise from Sabby. The premises were large, well furnished, very comfortable and had a large balcony. There was also a large TV which, for the rest of our stay in Canada, kept Martin absolutely spellbound.

We soon became close to a family, also from England, who lived in the apartment next door and had arrived in Canada a week before we had. The husband was a doctor at the nearby clinic and Dorothy, his wife, was from the north of England and was a born again Christian. It was through this family, their care for others and their quite natural way of talking to God that I learned to feel close to God myself. Studying the bible, and discussing it with other people, I began to feel that whatever the future held for us God was really with us. I still feel his support to this day.

After five or six months in the apartment we had decisions to make about our future. Dorothy and her family were ready to leave Toronto and travel north to carry out spiritual work, so that made us consider whether we should stay in Canada or return to England. The lease on the apartment could be renewed or cancelled, it was up to me. I had just applied for, and got, a job as a pedicurist at the Sheraton Hotel and was due to start in a week. How I got the job was a mystery to me, the only thing I knew about pedicury was it was something to do with feet! But with Dorothy about to leave and our futures up in the air it was time to make some firm decisions. To stay or go. Another part of the dilemma was that our house in the UK had been rented out for twelve months, and I'd had the full years rent in advance. So returning to it could well not be an option. I also spoke to the local travel agent regarding fares to England, and availability of seats, and was shocked and dismayed at how much the cost had risen.

Important decisions to make. We prayed for guidance.

I suddenly had a call from the travel agent. She had remembered my call and had kept our phone number. She told me that , due to a cancellation, she had four seats on a cheap charter flight to Heathrow the next day and they were ours if we wanted them. The cost, considerably less than a regular flight, was exactly equivalent to the cash we had left. It didn't take long to make up our minds so the answer was yes. "You see" said Dorothy "the Lord never lets you down". She was right.

So we said our goodbyes to Dorothy and her family and left for our return. Our sadness at leaving her was compounded when we got to the airport. We had decided that we would smuggle Sabby the cat back to avoid quarantine. We had given him a strong sleeping pill, wrapped him in an old sweater and hidden him in my hold-all. Unfortunately the flight was delayed for several hours and Sabby woke up howling, rather prematurely. Caught out we had to leave him with a friend who had come to see us off. It was very upsetting for all of us to hear his howling and to see him walking on "drunk" legs as he was taken away, but more so for Sara as he was her "little love". What was ironic on our arrival at Heathrow was that there was a strike of customs people which meant, had the flight been on time, we would have been able to smuggle him through!

We had been worried, before leaving Canada, about where we would live but I felt somehow that the house would be empty and so it proved, the tenants having moved out without leaving a forwarding address. I had therefore arranged for a friend, Jill, to meet us at the airport who had kindly agreed to take us home. We all piled into her mini and set off. On the way there Jill told me not to go on about God and his miracles quite so fervently " People will think you are crazy, not that they don't already, with you dashing off to the far side of the world!"

As we entered the house the phone started to ring. It was an old friend phoning to say hello and see how we all were. "See a miracle" I said to Jill.

Jill stayed on and helped us unpack and get the house back to some semblance of order. In the evening we went to a local Chinese restaurant to celebrate our return, said our farewells to Jill and returned to the house where we fell on our beds, jet lagged and exhausted.

The children returned to their respective schools and after a few teething problems caught up and settled in. I meanwhile had to face the reality, yet again, of finding a job and earning some money.

With very few opportunities locally I applied for a position in the City of London as a buyer and seller of money. I remember thinking at the time that whilst I knew a lot about spending it I did not know much, if anything, about buying and selling it.

At the interview I sat before a board of eight serious middle aged to elderly city men, all no doubt seeped in the world of money. They explained the job although I had

51

little idea of what they were talking about and tried to make a good impression. To my utter amazement it worked and they offered me the job. Furthermore the salary was frightening. At the time the national average wage was about two thousand or so pounds. They were offering me a salary of over forty thousand!

Still a little nonplussed I accepted the job, shook hands all round, and told them I was looking forward to working with them.

When I left I realized that getting the job was one thing, doing it quite another. I knew that I could only bluff my way so far and that the job was really beyond me. So I wrote them a letter to thank them but that I had also received another offer of employment which I felt I couldn't refuse. They replied to say how sorry they were that I would not be joining them and wished me every success in my new position.

NINE

Lovers were in my life, but no one special. And I always kept the children clearly and honestly in the picture about any of the men that were about. I did not want them to worry about what was, or wasn't, going on.

I tried my luck with a Jewish marriage bureau with rather chequered results. One of the first "gentlemen" they arranged for me was Alex. I wasn't too sure at first but he had a Rolls Royce and spoilt the children with presents. He wanted to marry me from the very first moment he saw me. "Darlink" he would say in his thick mid European accent "I am overwhelmed". He wore a wig which was always lopsided and which, for some unknown reason, he sprinkled with salt. Perhaps he thought it looked like dandruff, therefore making the wig appear natural. He also plied me with never ending presents, usually plants that wouldn't die. Before Alex my plants always died but his didn't and the house was overflowing with the damned things.

At the time I had no real job or income, apart from the widows benefit which by now had risen from eighteen pounds to twenty pounds a week. I was still paying off Ivan's debts and the mortgage payments often went unpaid. Knowing this the children thought that Alex was the only, and therefore the best, bet. I didn't agree.

I finally walked out on him one evening in a kosher restaurant. I'd just had a plate placed in front of me piled high with tongue and fattening potato latkas. At the time Alex was offering me the front seat in the synagogue "next to the Rabbi's wife, my darlink". The thought appalled me. I didn't want a claustrophobic, convenient marriage to a man I didn't love. I'd already tried that. Since Ivan's death two years before I had tasted freedom and although life was hard and a challenge at least it was my challenge. I wanted a different way of life and I wanted the children to develop with me, away from the narrow mindedness of the ordinary.

After Alex I decided that as I'd paid my fees to the Marriage bureau I might as well see what else they had on offer. Who knows, the right man for me might show up, I thought. How wrong could a woman be?

The bureau arranged for me to go to their premises in Goldhurst Terrace to meet a new "candidate", which suited me, being just ten minutes away from where we were living. I arrived, slightly early, to be met by Mrs Franks from the bureau and to be told about the man I was to meet. She started off by telling me he was an Israeli Rabbi. I told her I didn't want a rabbi, just a good Jewish husband. That's what I had paid my fee for. "Ah yes" said Mrs Franks "Don't worry, he'll love you". My immediate thought was that's all very well but will I love him. Mrs Franks continued "He's thirty three, the new breed out there. He's not fanatically religious, very new, very controversial"

"So why has he come to London?" I replied "I hear there are lots of widows in Israel, all desperate for husbands"

Mrs Franks response to my query was to carry on regardless. "His wife died, leaving him with seven children." I did the maths very quickly realizing I would have an instant family of ten children plus a husband.

"I think he needs a maid not a wife" I said " Forget it Mrs Franks. I am not interested in your new breed of Rabbi"

"Don't be hasty" replied Mrs Franks " He knows you have children and he'll send them all, his and yours, to a Yeshiva to study the Talmud."

I had the preposterous thought of my children going to a Yeshiva, with sideburns and that religious pale look. They wouldn't do it. They'd kill me first.

"Mrs Franks, why not give him to a Yeshiva girl, he's not for me" I said as I turned to leave.

"Wait, wait. Not so hasty. He's handsome, over six feet tall. I could fall for him myself!"

"Well, why don't you, if he's such a catch?" I enquired, thinking to myself that if I was in her line of business I'd keep the best for myself

" Hymie wouldn't like that, dear"

"Who's Hymie? The Rabbi?"

"No, my Hymie." Said Mrs Franks "We've been married thirty five years. The Rabbi's yours with my blessings. Mazeltov"

I was incensed. "You're a disgrace to women" I shouted "I'm leaving. In fact I want a transfer to the gentile side of the business, it must be a sight better than yours"

At that moment the door opened and in walked a dream of a man. Tall, slim, black eyes, black beard, faded jeans and a badge covered denim jacket.

" Ah" said Mrs Franks brightly "This is Shlomo"

The Rabbi! And certainly a new breed of Rabbi alright. Well, well, well I thought , as you're here I might as well give you a go! Forgetting the Yeshiva and the ready made family of ten I shook hands and smiled warmly. As it turned out a little too warmly perhaps.

I was pushed in to the living room and the Rabbi led me straight to the couch. He was strong, powerful and very magnetic. He only spoke Hebrew but as I knew a little I was able to follow what he was saying to a certain extent. It appeared to me that he not only needed a maid for the ten children and for himself, but he needed money. I don't know if Mrs Franks knew that but if she did I don't know why she thought I was the right person for him. All I had was the flat, but perhaps she thought that was enough.

Realizing the situation was impossible I got up to leave. As soon as I did he pushed me back down until I was laying full length on the couch. He held me down and whispered in Hebrew to me "Open your legs for the Rabbi, in the name of God". I was terrified. I could only suppose that if he wasn't going to have me for a wife he thought he'd get what he could from the deal. With one hand pinning me down and the other at his fly he managed to get his body between my legs.

"Open your legs for the Rabbi" he demanded. I screamed loudly and tried to fight him off.

Hymie Franks must have heard me but as he came into the room the rabbi was off me as quick as a flash. I left quickly.

Later, when I called Mrs Franks to complain she was very apologetic. She said she couldn't check everybody out, could she. Perhaps he wasn't really a Rabbi.

Unfortunately he had my phone number from Mrs Franks and my address. He phoned me to say he was going to call round with some cakes by way of apology. I told him not to. He didn't call with the cakes but he did call again a further couple of times until I threatened him with the police if he bothered me again. Luckily he didn't.

No more bureaus for me – ever!

TEN

The children were all round my bed – the only place for chats, coffees and important decision making. We came to the conclusion that we should sell the house and move into a more interesting inner London area where I would, hopefully, find it more easy to find a job.

We bought paint, rollers, brushes and all necessary paraphernalia and began the task of redecorating the house. Ashley and I, being the tallest, did the top of the stairs, Sara did the middle bit of walls whilst Martin, the smallest of us, was responsible for the lower parts of the stairs and walls. We had great fun. We tied a roller on to a broom handle in order to reach the very tops of the walls and into high corners and Ashley held on to me to stop me falling from the step ladder. I managed to do quite a good job of it even though I did paint over numerous dead flies and cob webs. I don't think we could be described as the most professional of decorators but the house looked pretty good to us when we had finished. Apart, that is, from the results of a tin of paint which one of us had knocked down the stairs from top to bottom. It took a bit of time but with a lot of hard work and turpentine we managed to clear it up. Job done.

At that time I had a friend, Stephen, who was someone I could talk to about just about anything. Jobs, life, men, etc. He was an architect and a property investor on a small scale. He bought small terraced houses in poorer districts of London and rented rooms to students and a motley selection of people who could only afford a bed sitter way of life. From the money he made from the rents he was able to buy more houses and repeat the process. He told me that I should do the same and that I could make a lot of money by doing so. Occasionally I would go with him to collect his rents. His tenants were a mixed bunch. A couple of labourers from a local building site; a schoolteacher; a couple people who didn't appear to work but still always managed to pay their rent on time; an ancient woman of indeterminate age, a girl who was on the game, whose room cost her a little bit more than the others! I didn't like these rent collecting trips as they always made me feel uneasy and over privileged. They certainly made me think that I could never let rooms and collect rents for my own gain.

Then everything seemed to happen over a period of a week or two. We came to the decision to sell the house and very quickly Ashley found a buyer.

And then Stephen asked me to marry him. Up to that point I hadn't made love with him but when I did I thought that I had found love. I was happy. The children all liked him so they were happy. And Stephen's parents, Vera and Charlie, were happy. Everybody was happy. It was to be the start of yet another bizarre period in my life.

ELEVEN

Plans were made and the future mapped out. Our house was to be vacated in March (it was then the end of January) and we would move to Stephen's house. We would be married in Paris, whilst his mother would look after the children, and our two cats.

Stephens house, a tall, dilapidated, narrow Victorian building, sandwiched between two trendy, newly done up houses, was in Regents Park, overlooking London Zoo, close to Hampstead and Primrose Hill. I found out later that it was conveniently placed for Stephen to indulge in an odd pastime – late night, naked, kite flying. I eventually found out when he actually asked me to accompany him, also naked. I refused!

It was also close to Camden Town with its hippies, junk markets, wholefood stores, locks and art filled warehouses. All a lot different from our suburban place. I loved the smells and the flavours of the place.

Unfortunately Stephen was not so popular with his, mostly middle class, neighbours who, to me, all seemed to be something in television or films. Not only was his house run down and uncared for but it was also rented out, apart from three rooms, to an assortment of hippy types who seemed to come and go at all times of the night and day.

Stephen was very warm to me and the children and showed all of us a lot of affection and attention. He would sit for hours with pencils and paper designing and planning reconstruction of our new home together. He also got us all interested in vegetarian food, being a lifelong vegetarian himself. His parents, Vera and Charlie would often visit for Sunday lunch, or we would visit them. Always for nut roast

– they were vegetarians as well. Vera and Charlie lived fairly close to a canal and we would all go to see them and go out on a narrow boat for the day. It was great fun helping to open and close the locks and drifting through the ever changing scenery.

One day Stephen took us to view some new townhouses just opposite his own house. They were very nice, seemed like a good investment and he decided to buy one and put down a deposit. Life was good. I even arranged interviews at local schools for the children and sold most of our furniture in advance of the impending move. It was two weeks to removal day and four weeks to the wedding.

Then Stephen disappeared.

It was his night to stay at my house but I was a little concerned as I hadn't had our normal daily, sometimes twice daily, phone call. We were to go out for dinner and whilst he was always very punctual that night he was late, very late. I phoned his mother who, although very close to him, didn't know where he was but was convinced he would show up. And no, she didn't want me to phone the police. The next few days were like a nightmare. I thought Stephen was dead. My good friends Simone, a teacher, and Mike, the doctor who had treated Ivan, both liked Stephen and, whilst upset and worried themselves, were a great comfort to me.

Nine days after he had disappeared a rather shamefaced Stephen resurfaced. He said he had gone to his house in Wales but found he couldn't write because there was a postal strike. I was so happy to see him alive that I didn't think to ask why he hadn't phoned. He said he had needed to be alone for a while and I believed him.

Removal day arrived and we were to go to Stephens old house, the new one was not to be ready for at least six months. When we got there Stephen was not there, which was a surprise, but we settled in as best we could. In the evening I took the children to Chalk Farm for a pizza but on our return there was still no sign of Stephen. I was beginning to feel bad again and worried about Stephen. I had no indication, until two weeks previously, that there was anything possibly wrong with him or our relationship.

Well after midnight he came home and I made him talk to me. I had to know what was wrong. He told me he had another girlfriend and had gone to Wales with her. He had had a relationship with her for all of the eighteen months he had been with me and on the night he didn't see me he was with her. She, apparently, was as shocked to hear about me as I was to hear about her. What a mess. Talk about Jeckyll and Hyde.

We talked and he cried. He told me that it was a life with me that he wanted and that the other woman meant nothing to him. It was then that he told me about the strange relationship concerning himself and his parents. His father, he said, had been a vicar and had molested him when he was about ten. Vera his mother had then left his father and run off with her own stepfather, Charlie. I was never too sure whether this was a valid reason for Stephen's behaviour or just an excuse he used to justify it. Either way it was all a real mess.

I had registered the children at the local school but had done so in Stephen's name, Roth, as were about to be married. The school had agreed that it was a good idea.

We were also due to go to Paris in three days to be married. We agreed that we would still go but not to marry.

I said we would wait until I had time to adjust to the situation which Stephen had revealed to me.

Unfortunately the situation did not improve. Stephen, for all his declaration of love for me, still visited the other woman twice a week. I decided that I couldn't stay with him and began to look for a job and a new home for me and the children. It was a very bad time, full of tension and worry. I lost a lot of weight.

I got a job in an Estate Agents office. About the same time Stephen offered to sell me one of his rental houses in Walthamstow for four thousand five hundred pounds cash. He said that I could receive the rental income and when I found somewhere to live I could use the rents to pay the mortgage on the new property, whilst being the owner of two properties. It all seemed to make sense to me.

I gave him the four thousand five hundred pounds , which was part of the proceeds from the sale of my house, and he handed over the keys. He then told me that it would need to stay in his name for six months for some reason to do with tax or something. He also told me that his other girlfriend was living there rent free but he had given her a months notice. He said I could have the rents from the other tenants straight away.

Life however is never so simple. Stephen began to bully me, even hitting me on one occasion after which he cried and said " Don't send me to school mummy. Stephen will be a good little boy". It was very strange, very worrying and very scary. He cancelled the purchase of the townhouse opposite, threatened to bring in more women. His behaviour was becoming increasingly erratic. I humoured him as best I could until such time as I could move out. I tried to look back over the time we had to see if

I could see any previous sign of our troubled relationship. Apart from the naked kite flying he had tried to involve me in he had also tried to get me to attend "swinging" parties with him. I had gone to one purely in order not to upset him. I had then gone to another where I realised it wasn't for me and left. It all made me wonder why I seemed to pick such odd men for relationships. Or did they pick me? Were all men odd?

My rental house in Walthamstow was also a problem as it was difficult to get the rents in, even more difficult to get the tenants out. I realized it would take time and effort to get any money from the enterprise.

TWELVE

I found a flat. It was affordable and in Hampstead, near the children's' school and away from the horror of Stephen. I still didn't have the deeds to the rental house in Walthamstow so I knew that for a time I would have to put up with him in my life until the house was legally and fully mine.

On the day we moved out of Stephen's house we made several trips in our old Citroen car which had enough room for our belongings and the few bits of furniture we had kept from our previous move. Luckily Stephen was out so that made things a lot easier. Finally we left the slummy house for the last time and finished our transfer to our new home. As we entered and closed the door behind us Sara said "It's going to be lovely here. It's just like a hotel"

I had taken out a bigger mortgage than I really needed to buy the flat so that I had enough money to make the flat in to the sort of home I wanted for us. I transformed it from a boring old ladies flat with a scullery into an exotic environment for us all. I found beautiful pieces of art nouveau, lovely scrubbed dressers and fancy Victorian chests. The children and I soon felt at home and happy.

To make our happiness complete Stephen at last gave me the deeds for the house and we were free of him and his problems for ever.

I had also overcome the problem with the tenants at the house, which we all referred to as "Pembar Avenue", and was able to choose my own people to rent the rooms. I found them by advertising in the papers and Martin, aged twelve, became very adept at answering the phone and dealing with the enquiries. Slowly, slowly all the rooms were rented out and I would drive over every two weeks to collect the rents, with Sara tagging along as moral support. It wasn't always plain sailing. A tenant who couldn't afford the rent one week; a leaking roof; someone wanting to leave before the agreed time; someone else wanted to stay longer than agreed; someone's girlfriend moving in; a whole family moving in with a father who'd rented a room. There was always something happening. So much so that I began dreading going there. One tenant decided he was a vampire whilst his girlfriend declared herself a witch. They had seemed quite normal when they came to see about the room but when I went to collect the first months rent they were made up and dressed in their respective regalia. To make matters even more weird they kept a rat called Angela and it became a ritual that I would have to have a conversation with Angela – albeit a little one sided – before they would hand over their rent. Sara was spared the experience because she said she was allergic to fur.

After the trauma of collecting the rents Sara and I would be hungry and "in funds" so we would invariably go to a local Indian or Greek restaurant in Camden Town to relax, laugh and talk. Sara was fifteen and great company.

When we arrived home Ashley and Martin were always interested to hear the latest "Pembar" saga, particularly the vampire and the rat. I would retire to bed, in the room I shared with Sara, and they would sit round and listen. It was a large room with room for a chest freezer stocked with exciting and exotic foods. Martin would bring the coffee and entertain us with his clever and amusing mimickings.

Unfortunately life wasn't all laughs. The rent money, amounting to over £50 every two weeks when everybody paid, I used to keep in a coffee tin and referred to it as "the money for thrills not bills". Actually it more often than not was used to pay the bills. Even so with the rents from Pembar Avenue, my widows pension and small jobs – plus, more importantly, an unlimited overdraft - we lived well. Notwithstanding, I still had lots of financial problems.

I was over extravagant, forever taking us all out for meals, paying for trips abroad. I kept a very good wine cellar and had a passion for expensive way-out clothes. I developed a taste for art and would go to Christies and Sothebys, often bidding successfully for a treasure to bring home. Deep down I knew I was living in a fool's paradise, a view confirmed by my friends continually telling me that living on an overdraft was not a clever thing to do. I would often pay my bills on postdated cheques. Sara was appalled by my extravagance, as were all my friends. They were all worried about my behaviour and where it would end.

My theory was "Darlings, if you die without an overdraft you just haven't lived." I believed that then and, to a great extent, I still believe it. I believe in "The Life". And now, after all these years, Sara is no longer appalled and understands "The Life" - and overdrafts. One thing I do remember about Sara and our life then was one day when she and I were sitting in our bedroom she looked up from the paper she was reading and said "I'm just reading about one parent families and it's funny but I don't feel we are one". That was something. I'm pleased to say that my children were, and still are, mentally and emotionally strong. They all have style.

The children's education was a very important factor as well in our lives. Ashley was doing well at

William Ellis Grammar School in Highgate where he worked hard and was expected to get a place at Cambridge to read law. Subsequently he did just that and then went to the bar at Grey's Inn. We were all so proud of him. Not only was he a good scholar but was also quite a little business man in his spare time. During school holidays he worked as a milkman and the became a foreman. He bought chickens when they were at their cheapest, stored them in our bedroom freezer, and then sold them when the prices rose for a good profit. He used to get up and go to work so early in the morning that I told him to leave the house through his bedroom window so as not to disturb us. Luckily for him we lived on the ground floor so it wasn't too much of a problem. He also used to give me ten pounds a week to help with the housekeeping but I bought an original Louis Wain painting with it instead for three hundred and fifty pounds, still using postdated cheques I might add! Some years later I gave it to him as a wedding present. I understand it is now worth a few thousand pounds, a tangible reminder of the past.

Martin, on the other hand, was a bit of a problem. He was at the same school as Ashley but his work ethic was the complete opposite. He was quite moody, often depressed and frequently truculent. Sara and Ashley were worried about him. Martin and I were often alone in the house together when the other two had left which was lovely as we got on so well together. But Ashley would point out to me that all I did was to indulge Martin by sitting and listening to him complain and then take him out to dinner, often with wine. As Ashley said Martin was thirteen, potentially good at school and could get into Oxford if he applied himself and worked a little harder. He was right. Martin was very talented inasmuch as he could write well and act and was a talented painter and sculptor. But he lost interest in art and would only periodically produce anything. "He's wasting his time, Mum" said Ashley. I had lots of long talks with Martin, often resorting to emotional blackmail. I said he could leave school at sixteen and be a "nothing" or could do something to be proud of for his father's sake. "Why?" would be Martin's response.

Someone suggested to me that a public School might be the answer so I investigated the possibilities. We were living in the Borough of Barnet and they had a policy whereby boys of promise, but not necessarily money, whose parents were ratepayers in the borough, often were offered scholarships or financial assistance to attend Harrow School. I got the OK from the council and managed to get an interview for Martin at the school. He wasn't very keen on attending Harrow or going to the interview but along we went and he managed to get in. Although the fees were partially subsidised by the council it was still expensive for me and the good old overdraft came in handy once again.

One year Martin asked Sara and me to attend the school open day and instructed us to "dress up". We were pleased to be asked as it was an indication to us that Martin was taking an interest in his education at last. We both had lots of dressing up clothes so we did as he asked. I have to say but we both looked terrific, Sara particularly as she tottered along on a pair of my extremely high heels. We filled our hamper (the same one that transported Sabby the cat to Canada) with sandwiches, loaded it in the mini and off we went.

Open day at Harrow is quite an occasion! Rolls Royces; well stocked hampers; champagne; top hats; Lord and Lady this and that; housemasters and their families; cucumber sandwiches and strawberries and cream. The boys in boaters and tails with flowers in their buttonholes, although Martin seemed to be the solitary boy without a flower as his buttonhole was torn.

Martin surprised us with his enthusiasm, particularly for the grounds and the buildings, and said he wanted to show us the swimming pool. "Goody" we thought, he's taken up swimming, he's got an interest at last. We followed him through barbed wire fences and across muddy fields, jumped over small streams and avoided numerous cow pats, Sara wobbling along precariously in my shoes. I couldn't avoid laughing at our cross country ramble, made all the more memorable by Martin's appearance. I had bought his school uniform tails to last so they were slightly larger than they needed to be. This allied to the fact that he was not too tall meant that the tails reached down to the heels of his shoes, almost to the ground. He looked like a cross between Groucho Marks and Dustin Hoffman. At this particular moment as we trudged through the mud, Groucho was more in evidence.

Eventually we climbed up some steps leading to a fence where Martin crouched, looked through a hole, turned to us and said, excitedly, "Look, it's the swimming pool". Sara looked through the whole and said "It's lovely". My turn next. "Do you swim often, Martin?" I asked as I straightened up.

"Never" was his reply. Sara and I looked at each other, rather nonplussed.

After climbing over some further rubble, which Martin explained, was to be the new wing it suddenly started to rain quite heavily so we retired to the mini for cover and to eat our lunch. After that we all went to the local Sainsburys – tails and all.

Martin became a leading actor at the school and a leading practical joker. Some of his escapades were expensive for me, one in particular. The housemaster called me "Mrs Levinson, Martin has taken potassium pomangade".

I was aghast "Is he OK? Is he dead?"

"No, he stole it. Not swallowed it. And he's turned all the school water violet"

Initially I was relieved that Martin was safe but the relief turned to horror when I found out how expensive it was to reverse the process of dyeing water.

Martin eventually left school at eighteen but not to attend university. Instead he became a very successful free lance copywriter and designer working for various advertising agencies in London. He earns well but is still cynical and funny.

"Loves his work and his Mum" he once told me. He is a happy man.

What more can I ask for?

THIRTEEN

A different scenario was about to take shape. Another ad appeared in the evening paper for medical reps. The job was easy to get to, a training course offered and the children were now old enough, and therefore easier, to leave. I applied and was given an interview, after which I was offered the job.

I went to a lovely old hotel in Surrey for the six week, intensive training course and found the other people on the course all very nice and great fun. The standard of the training was very high and everything about the company was professional and ethical, both on the course and later when I started to work with them. They seemed to like my individual style of dressing and speaking, even allowing me the privilege of going "off script" and using my own presentation rather than sticking to the company prescribed words, as most of the others reps were trained to do. This gave me confidence – not something I lacked too much of anyway – and helped me be successful, and happy, in the job.

I liked the work, was successful and made some really good relationships with a lot of the doctors I dealt with, some of them even becoming firm friends. I was given a large, brand new company car but when the regional manager saw my driving he immediately arranged for me to choose a much smaller car of my choice – and definitely automatic.

I was initially given most of North London as my "patch" but later, as I became more successful, I was given a very prestigious area in W1 which included Harley Street, Wimpole Street and Knightsbridge. Very exclusive. I also believed quite firmly that the expensive clothes I favoured gave me the appearance of style and quality which gave the doctors I dealt with a level of confidence in me and in what I told them.

An interesting and enjoyable part of the job was entertaining groups of doctors and their wives where we would show them a short medical film, give them a short medical talk and then have a lovely dinner on a grand scale. Because of my Central London area I was allowed a free hand with the invitations, venues, menus and table plans. I always invited a few non medical people – usually friends – and often one of the children. My regional manager, Colin, loved these evenings and would always bring his wife along who loved them as well. A fellow rep, Miles, would help me on these occasions to give me a little moral support and a lot of physical support. He and I were good friends and he often joined me on my rent collecting visits to Pembar Avenue when the children were unable to do so. We always had dinner together on rent collecting nights and I cannot recall him ever missing one of these evenings.

Miles was thirty four when I met him, I was thirty seven. He was desperate to find a woman to marry and have a family. I was always fixing dates for him, usually unsuitable ones, and in the end he got quite upset with my choice of potential marriage candidates and swore never to meet any more. He told me he thought they were all "horrible". He said he'd sooner stick to riding, being the owner of half a horse. I thought it was amusing when I asked him which half and he told me it was the half that ate!

His area of responsibility was immediately next to mine and when convenient we would have breakfast together. We would sit and put the world to rights, discuss common "sales" problems and I would complain about the awful letters I got from the electricity board or the rates people complaining about non payment. When we'd finished we hadn't made a single doctor call and it was more often than not time for lunch. We both liked American style burgers so we would have an enjoyable lunch and then put it down on expenses, creating a fictitious doctor who needed entertaining in a bid to convince him to buy our products. Colin, the regional manager, knew of our "illegal" activity and even on occasions, would join us. All great fun.

During this period I was having a relationship with an Austrian called Geoffrey. He was a lovely exuberant man, a lover of the arts and a lecturer. He loved me, my home, my cooking, my children, my friends, my style. In fact he loved my everything. He proposed, bought me a beautiful diamond ring, and we got engaged. We celebrated by having a lovely party, which Sara and I organised and prepared. The house was full of friends and we all had a great time.

Lovely as he was Geoffrey had one major fault. He was never on time for anything. It was very annoying and I began to get very frustrated by him until eventually I felt I just couldn't spend my life sitting around waiting for him. He'd phone, often repeatedly, to say "I'm on the way" but still be hours late. Late dinners, theatre performances missed, meals ruined, journeys delayed. After eighteen months of "waiting" I decided enough was enough and, sadly, I ended the relationship. He was a lovely man but that was that. I gave him back his diamond ring.

Everyone said I was mad. I probably was.

FOURTEEN

At one of the many evening dinners I arranged for doctors a strange coincidence happened. I had set up the tables and made all the arrangements for the forty doctors I had invited, made sure the flowers on each table were all in place. The guests began to arrive. One doctor came in alone. "Norman" I said "What an unexpected pleasure. How nice to see you. Come and sit on my table". I hadn't seen Norman for some time and he seemed delighted to see me and the welcome I gave him. At the close of the dinner I gave one of my zany "sales" speeches, which seemed to appeal to Norman considerably. We sat and drank and talked and I invited him to come to the house to eat the following week and he accepted wholeheartedly.

Over dinner the next week, at which I intended to catch up on old times with him, it became apparent very quickly that he was not the man I thought he was. He was a completely different Norman. We laughed at my "mix up" and at how much he resembled the Norman I had thought him to be. But out of the coincidence and the confusion a long and difficult relationship was born. Norman told me that he had fallen in love with me almost as soon as he saw me and our relationship developed into one full of fun, love and laughter. We had some interesting times along the way. One concerned a rather weird experience with a ouji board.

Norman and I were hosting a dinner party at his flat in Islington. Our guests were Jane and Frank and Peter and Isadora. Jane had been a prostitute and would often regale us with interesting – and amazing – stories about her working life but gave up the profession when she married. Her husband, Frank, was a doctor in New Zealand but they were in London for a year on an exchange and lived along the road from Norman.

Peter and Isadora lived in Ascot, he an estate agent, she ran her own business knitting items for Harrods and Selfridges.

It was getting late when Jane, who also claimed to be a white witch, said she wanted to play the ouji board. I don't think any body else believed in such stuff but we said OK. So we cut out pieces of paper with the alphabet on them and placed them around the round table at which were sitting. We found a glass and settled. Jane explained we should all place a finger on the glass and see where it went around the table.

The glass seemed to move on its own volition, slowly at first but then in an uncontrolled and alarming manner. To my horror the glass spelled out I.V.A.N. and then spelled out a number of swearwords, refused a beer and called me a "COW" and Norman a "POOF". No one in the room, apart from Norman, knew of my first husband and I was utterly amazed. How on earth did it happen?

The glass then slowed down a bit and spelled out the fact that Enid Blyton was in trouble with Noddy. All a bit mysterious until a day or so later Enid Blyton's book were banned in libraries for being a bad example to children.

Finally, before becoming completely immobile, the glass spelled out a very strange story. It concerned a child called Kim, whose parents were Kevin and Dorothy. Kim told us she had a dog called Stephen and a doll named Jennifer.

Kim told us she was six years old and had been run over by a bus and killed at Christmas. She was sad and kept telling us she missed, and kept asking for, her mummy, daddy and her dog. She said she lived in Welwyn in Hertfordshire.

All very mystifying and goose bump making.

The dinner party broke up. Frank and Jane walked the few steps to their house in which they were staying and Peter and Isadora drove back to Ascot.

Norman went into a deep depression and wouldn't see me for over a month.

Intrigued by Kim's story I checked with the Welwyn police the following day to see if it had actually happened and, after checking their files, they confirmed that indeed it had. Fifty years ago at Christmas. Amazing!

Norman strange moods happened a lot and often created a lot of sorrow and upset.

He came to see me one day, bringing with him a rabbit for me to cook. It was special, he said, because it had been given to his father, also a GP, by a patient who had shot it whilst on a hunt. I put the "special" rabbit in the oven and because I needed to go out, left a note for Sara to let her know it was there for dinner. I arrived back a little later to find Norman distraught and hysterical. "They've eaten my rabbit! Your lot have eaten my rabbit. It was special! My father gave it to me! It was mine!". I didn't help the situation by seeing the funny side and laughing. I told Norman he could have steak and I would buy him another rabbit for another day. It didn't help.

"I don't want another one. I wanted that one. I told you it was special. My father gave it to me" Norman wailed, and left in a huff.

Unfortunately that wasn't the only "foodie" occasion to show Norman in a different light. It was his birthday one New Years Eve and I'd agreed to cook a duck for him in the way he particularly liked. Just after I had put it in the oven, at about six o'clock, the phone rang. By sheer coincidence, it was my good friend, Nora, telling me not to eat as there would be lot's of food at her party which we were going to later that night. I told her I was just cooking a duck specially for Norman but she said I should take it out of the oven and save it for the following day. I agreed and phoned Norman. He was not pleased. "You promised" he shouted petulantly "It's my birthday. I've been looking forward to my duck all week !" I told him we would be eating at Nora's and could eat it tomorrow. "I don't want to eat out. I want duck. You promised!" I relented, took the duck from the fridge and put it back in the oven. But the saga continued. The phone rang again. This time it was a friend, Simone, who was also having a party that night to which were going after Nora's.

I told her the story of the duck, Norman's tantrum and my predicament. She told me not to spoil Norman and to take the duck from the oven and to eat it tomorrow. I did and phoned Norman immediately and told him. He was so furious that I agreed to put the poor duck back in the oven. The third time I had done so.

Sara, who had seen and heard the whole troublesome episode then joined in.

"You're mad! Why cook now, get the smell of it on you, when you have to go to two parties at which you will be fed. It's ridiculous and quite selfish of Norman. I won't have any respect for you if you give in to him. Don't spoil him. It's common sense to eat it tomorrow. He's lucky to get it anyway, the way he carries on. Put the bloody thing back in the fridge". I did.

Norman and I had a miserable time at both parties and the next day, instead of cooking the duck, I threw it out. At the time it was not funny but now I cannot fail to smile whenever I cook duck.

Norman's petulance came to a head when I told him I was pregnant. I was 41 and he was 35 and he reacted by leaving me.

I took his actions remarkably calmly, being content with the knowledge of the child in me. It made me feel young and womanly. He would occasionally come and see me but would never discuss my condition or the situation. He said he wanted to remain friends forever but we stopped being lovers.

Seven weeks into my pregnancy Norman came to see me one evening. He was warm and touched my belly. He kissed me and left. A little later that evening I started to bleed and miscarried, although I didn't seem to have any emotional response at the time. I didn't tell Norman for a few days and when I did he came over to see me. He was very quiet and licked his lips continually, a habit I knew from experience meant he was very stressed. We didn't say much and he didn't stay long but after he left I sat and cried and cried and cried. The realisation of the loss of the new unborn life hit me at last and I felt so alone, tired and forlorn.

My whole life seemed to be weighing me down. My relationship with Norman was changed irrevocably and although he came to stay with me occasionally we never made love. The children were all away from home. My job had lost its challenge and its enjoyment and I was tired and bored. I felt like a hamster on the wheel of life paying bills, eating, working, sleeping and just going round and round again and again.

I realized I had to change my life and get out of the circle of despair I was in and that was what I planned to do.

What actually happened wasn't part of the plan at all.

THE WRONG MAN

The woman was a medical rep. She held dinners to entertain her potential clients. She'd made all the arrangements. Dressed all the tables with flowers and cigarettes. Her guests began to arrive when she saw a man she knew from some time ago. A doctor. She welcomed him and said how unexpected it was to see him. He was alone so she asked him to join her at her table. He was delighted to do so. She was interested in him straight away. He in her. He said later it was love at first sight. The lady gave her customary post dinner sales pitch and the man was mesmerised. They sat and ate and talked and flirted. She invited him to visit her the next week at her home and share a meal with her. He did.

Over dinner it became obvious to the woman that the man was not the man she had thought him to be. He was a different doctor. He was the wrong man. But a relationship started. A relationship that was both long and difficult in many ways.

The woman told the man she was pregnant but he appeared not to care and left her for several weeks. She accepted this and was content with the knowledge of the child within her. He came to visit sometimes but they never talked of her pregnancy or their relationship. They stopped being lovers but he wanted to stay her friend.

When she was seven weeks pregnant the woman began to bleed and lost the baby. She felt unmoved by the fact. She told the man a few days later about the loss and he came to see her. She appeared calm whilst he was with her but after he left she cried uncontrollably for a long time.

She realized how great the loss of a new unborn life could be. She felt tired, slow and heavy.

The relationship between the man and the woman continued but it was changed forever. They never made love. She felt like a hamster on an everlasting wheel of boredom and pointlessness.

FIFTEEN

Saturday 13th November 1976 started out very much the same sort of day as any other, but was the beginning of something I could not have envisaged.

Norman and I were having dinner at the Royal Hotel, Kensington with new friends Ben and his wife. Ben was the food and beverage manager at the hotel so we got the red carpet treatment. Not that it helped with the food we got. Everything that was meant to be cold was warm and everything that was meant to be hot was cold.

The conversation wasn't too hot either until after the meal when the conversation took a turn for the better and I began to view the "food and beverage" manager in a completely different light. All he seemed to want to talk about was sex.

Norman was not too impressed by this change in tone and wanted to leave. I however unknowingly, had thoughts planted in my mind about Ben that, whilst initially dormant, would eventually flower into life.

The weekend passed until, at five o'clock on Monday evening, there was a knock on the front door. Opening it I was confronted by Ben saying "Shalom". He, his wife, mother in law and two children all lived two floors above us in the same block of flats so were in the habit of using the same entrance to the building as we did. Ben told me he hadn't stopped thinking about me since Saturday night and asked if he could come in for a drink. I felt slightly awkward but also flattered. Norman was very fussy about his drinks, especially as he paid for them all, and I was a little nervous of using them. Amongst the bottles however was a bottle of blackcurrant liqueur which I could water down to disguise its use. It was very strong, tasting like Benylin expectorant at first but over Ben's subsequent and frequent visits it got weaker and weaker. Ben however didn't notice. His mind, above all things, was on sex! And in his mind it involved me!

After a number of visits I decided I should make things clear to him, perhaps shock him into realizing the situation "Look, Ben, I'm not going to fuck you, you know!" He was shocked and made it clear that no woman had ever turned him down so bluntly. Poor wife, I thought. He had obviously tried it on with a number of women before me. Just like a man, I thought, and asked him to leave when he had finished his weak Benylin. Although I kept refusing him I have to say I felt faintly flattered. After all he was thirty two and I was a widow of forty, albeit, an attractive one I thought.

The very next night he was back. I was waiting for Norman to arrive when there was a knock on the front door. I knew immediately who it was and stayed in the kitchen, refusing to answer the door. The knocking continued and, feeling silly about hiding from him I eventually opened the door. He appeared to want to talk but suddenly grabbed me in a masterful way and kissed me passionately. I endured it, even enjoyed it, perhaps for slightly longer than I should but then pushed him away. I reminded him that his wife was upstairs and Norman would be arriving at any minute. He had another Benylin and then left.

The next day he phoned. He was beginning to be a real problem. The friends who I had told advised me to have nothing to do with him. It was all too close to home and I should consider Norman and Ben's wife.

A couple of days later he knocked again. I really had begun to dislike him by then and because I didn't want to be compromised I threatened to tell his wife. In response he bought me a present. A small white cotton hanky. He stayed, as usual, for his usual Benylin, which reminded me that it needed to be watered down again to hide its use from Norman. Ben then moved from the hard dining room chair to the soft and comfortable couch in the lounge. He invited me to join him. I refused to do so and in response he stood up and gave me a mind blowing kiss. We talked and I was beginning to think that he did have a soul and a mind and was perhaps a nice guy, when I thought "No, it's only because he wants to get me into bed" He asked me if I was flattered and I said "No, men always want to screw me" (except Norman, I thought) "and I never do, except in exceptional circumstances".

He found out that Norman wasn't always with me on Mondays and wanted to come for a meal, make love and then go home to his wife. All I wanted was for him to leave me alone so I said OK. He was to come at three and go home at twelve.

On the Friday I went shopping with Ben's wife, Dina, and Ben tagged along. I didn't wear any make up in an attempt to put him off. In the evening we went home to their flat to prepare for Shabbat. Dina lit candles and Ben made Kiddish and put some Mozart on. Ben had told me he was a lover of classical music and that it elevated and relaxed him. I left and returned to our flat in order to prepare Shabbat for Norman. By the time he got home the flat was warm, candlelit and freshly polished.

After we had eaten we went upstairs to see Ben and Dina for drinks. I didn't really want to go and again I did not wear make up. Ben hardly looked at me and whilst I felt good and hoped my make up subterfuge was working I did feel a small pang of regret. Deep down, though, I was relieved and made my decision to call the whole thing of with Ben.

Or at least meet him at his hotel and get it over and done with.

SIXTEEN

On the Sunday I visited Ivan's grave. It was the first time I had ever been but I felt it was the right time to do so. I needed and wanted to go. I told Ivan all about the children and even mentioned my "sexy" neighbour. I felt good after the visit and really glad I had been.

On the Monday I called Ben and called the whole thing off, told him not to come round. For one thing it was far too close to home and secondly, to be honest, I just couldn't be bothered. He tutted and said he would call back, which did and invited me to go for a walk with him. I wasn't keen to go. It was cold, looked like snow and I was trying to avoid being alone with him. He offered to take me for tea at his hotel and, foolishly, I thought why not. We arranged that I would drive to the hotel at three thirty and park the car in the car park. He said he would pay for it later.

I dressed in an expensive, older looking and sophisticated way. It made me feel too good and too old for him and I hoped he would see this, be put off, and leave me alone.

I met Ben and he escorted me to the large, opulent lounge overlooking the private road to Princess Margaret's apartment. We had tea and talked but I was bored and wishing very much that I had refused the invitation. After tea we walked through Hyde Park and he kissed me, as I knew he would. I again tried to tell him that we couldn't get involved, it would do damage to his family.

We returned to the hotel and he told me he had taken a suite. I really wanted to go home but relented and agreed to go to his room. All I could think about was just getting it over with, and hoping I wouldn't catch some terrible disease. At least pregnancy was off the agenda, I was on the pill.

I wanted to hurry the whole process up now and we took the lift to the penthouse on the tenth floor. When we got to the room I didn't know whether I should get into bed or look at the tremendous view of Park Lane. I knew which I would prefer! Ben appeared with a bottle of "good" wine but hadn't thought to bring a bottle opener. He phoned down to reception and asked for one but from memory I don't think it ever turned up. We both felt a little awkward. He fiddled with the heating whilst I stared out off the window, not knowing what to do. This was all a bit new for me.

He kissed me and I thought it only fair to respond in kind, even if I was only going to pretend to enjoy it. We were both undressed on the bed by now and kissing more passionately. His kisses were hot and devouring but I noticed his penis was still soft and flaccid. It crossed my mind that perhaps he hadn't had so many women as he boasted and just liked to talk about it. And then the situation change dramatically and the love making became quite intense and mind blowing. First we fucked and then we made love, kissing, touching, caressing. He entered me again and again. I climaxed twice, even faked a third just to please him. I even began to see him as a man I loved slightly, not the man upstairs or Dina's husband. He had a nice body and was warm, attentive and sensual. In fact he was a good screw!

When it was over we felt no embarrassment. I felt content and lay in his arms. It was a beginning, although I didn't realize that then. Had I done so I might have had the strength to walk away. But I didn't.

At eight o'clock we left the hotel and went to a pub in Kensington where we knew we would not be recognised. We ate. We kissed. We talked. How we talked. It was as if we had known each other for many lifetimes and we had no reservations, no boundaries.

I knew it was going to be a long, deep and painful love. There was no doubt we would fall in love, perhaps we already had in a way. Not only with our bodies but with our minds as well. We both understood that we would both gain and lose in the relationship. Ben told me he wanted to take up the challenge and that I was in his blood. We talked and kissed some more.

We went home to my flat went straight to bed and made magical love again. Afterward Ben went upstairs to Dina and I bathed and thought about what happened. I had never experienced such orgasms ever before or been so physical in my love making with anyone else. Ben had said that he wanted a proper relationship where we could meet and talk about things, not just for sex. He wanted to be my friend and take me to Israel and look after me. I believed him.

I felt physically and emotionally spent and I fell asleep, intensely and deeply.

I was awakened by the telephone ringing. It was Ben. We talked for a long time and he said he wanted to call down to see me a little later. But when he arrived he seemed to have changed. He'd apparently bumped into his mother in law who was on her way up to his flat to see Dina. I thought perhaps it had made him have second thought about us and that it was all over before it had hardly begun. I told him to leave because Norman was due home and that he shouldn't call or see me the following day because Norman was to be at home for a day off.

The next day, however, Norman had an extra appointment to go to so I phoned Ben to tell him. He seemed happy to hear from me and asked me to go to the hotel and have tea with him and we had a nice time. I still felt however, as I left the hotel. to go and meet Norman, that it was over.

When I arrived home I met Dina and her baby outside the flats waiting for a cab to take her to visit a friend, but when she saw me she asked if I could take her and cancelled the cab. I couldn't really say no, even though Norman was furious. What was to be a short trip down the road turned into a nightmare of a journey. Dina couldn't remember where her friend lived and we went round and round in circles. After about an hour of abortive searching we finally returned home.

That same evening Ben phoned to say that Dina had left a book in my car and when they returned home at about ten thirty would it be OK to call in and get it. I naturally said yes but Norman was very put out. He called them "bloody Israelis" and that they had a "bloody cheek". I told him it was my flat, I would do what I wanted and I would not be dictated to by him. He now said I was "bloody mad" and we ate our meal in a frosty silence. When we had finished I told him that I felt it would be better if he stayed at his own flat in Islington in the future. We had been together for over three years and there was still no sign of us being married, I said. He blustered for a while but then gave up and went to bed. By the time Ben called Norman was fast asleep.

Whilst Dina went up to their flat Ben and I went down to the car to retrieve the book. We kissed and wanted each other. He said we could meet at nine the next morning. I didn't think I could wait that long. I wanted him so much.

I went upstairs and ran a bath. As I lay in the warm water my thoughts were very erotic. Licking, kissing, touching, feeling, caressing, entwining into each other. I held nothing back. I touched myself as if I were him. I was on such a high I thought I would never come down. I wanted him so much.

Meanwhile Norman was snoring, disgustingly loudly, in the next room!

SEVENTEEN

I didn't know how far things would go, how long it would continue. I certainly didn't want to think about how it would end. Would it be deep, sexy, painful. How much misery or ecstasy would I endure, knowing full well that both would be present somewhere in the journey.

We met as often as we could and talked. I felt in his blood and I knew he felt in mine. We discussed the pain that we both knew would come at some point but we both wanted the affair to continue. We just couldn't stop.

One evening as I was dressing to go out to meet a girlfriend Ben turned up at my door, with an excuse about his daughter's lunchbox. It amused me as I didn't think he needed any excuses anymore. I invited him in and suddenly we were making love. We bathed together. Then, as usual, he left me to return to his own home and wife.

Things began to move quickly and strangely, as if by their own volition. I was loved by Ben, and he by me, and we saw each other every day. Our times together were full of warmth, conversation and love.

Norman and I were being effected by the whole thing and we were beginning to have our problems. He was going out more in the evenings and I was getting upset and retaliating by doing the same. Norman was also being effected by the fact he was placing his father in a mental hospital and was very upset by it. One evening I went to visit my cousin Sonia to have dinner and didn't return to the flat until two in the morning, which was very unlike me. Norman, surprisingly, was still awake and he was very annoyed. I knew I should have phoned and told him and shouldn't deliberately upset him. I felt like a traitor. I still loved Norman at the time and kept asking myself if that was so why was it I loved Ben so much and wanted him so badly. Was it because he offered me so much. I got the same care and attention he gave his wife and a love that was one hundred percent for me. We had long and deep conversations about religion, our problems, Norman, my work, the children. Just about everything in fact. He engulfed me in his family life and he was in mine. I was part of him, he was part of me. It was not just about sex any more. It was love.

Ben wanted to take me to concerts, take Norman and me on holiday. He wanted to take me to back to Judaism. He wanted to make love to me. He wanted to be with me. Me! He made me, for the first time in my life, feel my worth. I wanted, and had, a man I could confide in completely, talk to uninhibitedly and love deeply and sexually. That man was Ben.

As the days passed our love became all consuming. We saw each other every day and our love making became beautiful and smooth. Sensual and earth shaking. I felt sad, happy, emotional all at the same time. We had lots of laughter as well. One day Martin came home early and Ben climbed out of the bathroom window with his trousers undone. Martin, who knew about the whole thing, as did Sara and Ashley, said "It's not quite a scene from Mary Poppins, is it Mum?"

I used to go to the synagogue with Ben and he was so happy that I was becoming part of his Jewish life. He gave me red roses and more and more of himself. We listened to beautiful classical music together, danced intimately together in the bedroom where we made love, laughed and bathed together. Ben made me laugh by saying that he was worried that the excitement was too much for a woman of my age. He was worried that I would have a heart attack every time I had an orgasm!

One Christmas he gave me a beautiful gold Magen David (Star of David) whilst we were sitting in the car in Hyde Park. It was foggy so, as we felt somewhat protected, we took the opportunity to make love there and then. After we went home, where I was to join him and Dina for traditional Chanuka Doughnuts and wine. As I entered their flat my Jewish lover was praying and looked at each other and laughed quietly.

During this time Norman was in the process of leaving our flat completely. It was what I wanted. He had become so cold and barren. He seemed to give little but want a lot. It was strange how anti Norman I had become when I had loved him six weeks earlier. I questioned myself and my capacity for loving and feeling and how easily I had found it to give up Norman.

I remember once, when after making love at the hotel, Ben and I had gone for a meal at Lubas Bistro, behind Harrods. Until then I had felt that he still really belonged to Dina and his family. As we were sitting there he called me darling and asked me what I wanted to order. For some reason I suddenly felt we were a true "us" and that we belonged to each other.

I felt empty and restless when I wasn't with Ben and I know he felt the same. It made me feel strange and uneasy not being in control of my emotions. I could be sitting in a chair all alone and suddenly feel his presence so strongly it was as if he was touching me. I could feel his hands and his breath. I wanted him, needed him. I adored him. There would often be tears in my eyes and my heart.

Our lovemaking was still incredible. Ben could bring me to so many climaxes. One night he said it was twenty two! I used to go wild, wanted to jump out of the window. I masturbated with feathers, put fruit in my vagina which he would eat. He even poured wine inside me and sucked it together with the juices from my vagina. My love had turned me into a madwoman, obsessed with, and taken over, by sex.

And all the time Ben would tell me how much he loved me and would never leave me.

One night I made a meal and took it upstairs to share with Ben and Dina. After we had eaten Dina fell asleep in the chair, just a few feet from us. In our madness we made love there and then and I kept hoping that Dina was really asleep. I found out later that she had actually only pretended to be asleep. The next day Ben and I felt really bad about what we had done and began to worry that our love would one day destroy us.

I was forty and was experiencing something I never felt would, or could, happen. I never felt I could feel so much love for another human being and have it reciprocated.

Dina by now knew all about things, and she and Ben wanted me to move in with them. They also wanted me to have his baby. Dina was not jealous but strangely I was. Ben said that he and Dina no longer made love and I knew he was thinking of divorcing her and marrying me.. He said he still loved her in a special sort of way and didn't want to desert or abandon her. It made me feel that I should try and fall out of love with Ben and start to lead my own life again. When I told him how I felt it made him very sad and cried a lot. He was deeply upset, couldn't sleep or eat. He kept talking about marrying me but that also made him depressed. He had been married to Dina by his father, a Rabbi, and he didn't want to lose his father's respect.

One month I told Ben I was six days late and he was ecstatic. Almost immediately my period started but Ben said not to worry, we could try again.

I started to feel, once again, that we could have a future together. We talked about marriage again, sometime in the future. We had developed a constant rhythm between our minds as well as our bodies. We were wired together for ever. I felt that he lifted me up to heights I had never experienced and I loved him to the point of no return. I felt I would do anything for him and knew he felt the same. We were so very involved in each others lives and becoming more and more so as each day passed.

He said "This is the phenomenon called love. Write it down. I swear, I will never leave you"

EIGHTEEN

We watched the horse guard parade in Hyde Park, then went to a preview of Art Nouveau at Sotheby's. Ben then returned to the hotel.

When we met up later Ben said "My love, I've been ditched." I wasn't sure what he meant. "Sacked, my love. Sacked" we were both stunned, lost for words. He was so worried about what to tell Dina. I was so worried that this might be a first step in his return to Israel and away from me. My legs felt weak. We went for lunch to try and talk about what to do. I knew, as well, that his pride had been hurt very badly.

Norman was no help in the situation either. He knew about Ben and me and now only came to see me spasmodically. He was hurt by my infidelity which made him rude and aggressive. He would continually tell me, and Ben when he had the opportunity, to "Fuck Off". We both understood his reaction and both felt upset for him.

A month after he had been sacked Ben was finding it very hard to get another position. He went for a number of interviews and I often accompanied him but all were unsuccessful. The most common reaction was "Sorry, we don't hire Israelis". There was a growing possibility that he would have to return to Israel, something both Ben and I were very concerned about. Dina wanted me to go. Ben wanted me to go. It was a very bad time for all of us. He was desperate to find work in the UK or Israel seemed the only option for him.

I didn't think I could bear it if he left. I certainly considered the possibility of going with him but it wasn't the right time. Martin still had another year at school and I felt sick and upset about having to wait until the following year.

I had also promised Norman some time previously I would go to Crete with him for old time's sake and the trip was now imminent. I was desperately looking for a way of not going but Dina said it would be unfair to Norman not to. Whilst I was frantic about leaving Ben, particularly in the current awful situation, I felt I had no choice and Norman and I left for our holiday in Crete. As we did so Ben and Dina waved goodbye from their window. I could see Ben was crying. We hadn't been separated before and I called him from the station to say goodbye.

The holiday with Norman was the saddest, sickest, dazed weeks I had ever experienced. Every day seemed to contain three hundred and sixty hours. I couldn't eat, I couldn't sleep, I couldn't enjoy anything, I cried all day, every day. I thought I was going to die.

I phoned Ben nearly every day and, with mixed feelings, found him to be in the same state as me. I knew Dina was very worried about him. Norman was trying to be kind but I was sick. He said he wanted to be with me but it was too late for that. I was far too distant from him. I desperately wanted to get an earlier flight home but it was impossible. Every hour was insufferable.

Crete – 28th June 1977

My Darling
How I miss you, my beloved.
How sad and sick I am, how time just drags and drags into infinity.

The nights take me to hell.
Life without you, my loved one, is just existing, waiting
to die.
I spend all my time wishing I could fly home because
that is where you are.
Nothing can compensate for the lack of you

Love forever

It was my birthday, 26th June, and I was in a state of hysteria. We had travelled around the island but I hated every minute. The hours all passed like years and I had lost the capacity to smile. I still cried all the time. Poor Norman. Finally after a most excruciating time it was time to leave Crete and go back to where I belonged, to my life and to my love. The time seemed to pass more slowly on the journey back than it had whilst in Crete but at long last we were in the car home from the airport. I shook uncontrollably all the way but came alive as I rushed up the stairs to my love. Ben's face lit up with love and longing for me. Norman left for home and Dina gave us time together in my flat. We made sad love and vowed never to be apart ever again. We had both found it unbearably painful. We talked about our love, how disturbed we were by its depth and strength. What was going to happen. Ben had no job and Dina was so left out of his life now. The fear of him having to go to Israel was frightening and we realized that he had to find a job by July it would become a reality.

There was no job.

NINETEEN

Dina and the children went to Israel a week before Ben. He and I spent a magical five days and nights together. We agreed that he would go and look for a job and I would follow him in eleven days to spend three weeks with him. After he left I felt so empty. I cried all the time, even though he phoned several times a day.

The day of my departure arrived and Sara came with me to the airport to see me off. I was a strange mixture of apprehension and happiness. How were we all going to feel in a small apartment together? Would Ben find a job and actually stay in Israel? What did the future hold for us all? I went from thought to thought, from high to low several times as the miles and the time passed. Suddenly we were approaching the welcoming lights of Tel Aviv. Somewhere out there, I thought, my beloved man is waiting for me. As I left the plane the soft, warm air caressed my face and arms. I felt at home. I was in love and happy, excited and filled with emotion. Dina and Ben were waiting for me. Bens face radiated all that I was feeling. It was such a joy to be with him. Dina turned away as Ben and I threw ourselves into each others arms.

We went to Dina's Aunts flat in Kiryat Moshe, Jerusalem.

The holiday was fantastic and I was able to spend time with Ben. I would prepare meals and we would take them and eat on the balcony overlooking the old city of Jerusalem. It was idyllic. Ben went for interviews and I would meet him afterwards and we would walk and talk. One day he had an interview at the Dan Hotel in Tel Aviv and after we had lunch in old Jaffa overlooking the

Mediterranean. When we had eaten we lay on the cool grass and relaxed. We were so in love. At the same time we were sad and afraid. We held each other and cried.

Ben was offered the job at the Dan, the first chance of work in months, but he turned it down. Later I was to find out because he felt he wanted to try England again. He apparently also turned down other jobs in Israel for the same reason.

My time in Israel was coming to an end and Ben was desperate to find and buy a ring for me. He said it had to be just right. Eventually he found one and had a wonderful and moving time putting it on my finger at the Western Wall. A photographer took our photo and from then on Ben called me his wife.

Later the same day we had dinner at the Hilton, danced until late, and then, on the way back to the flat, made love in a parked, empty, red bus.

A number four.

DINA

Time in Israel with Ben and Dina, particularly Dina, was a real eye opener.

It was hard for me to believe this woman's complete lack of care for anyone, except herself. She hardly ever moved from her swing chair on the veranda, she was quarrelsome and demanding, particularly of Ben and me. Whenever a visit somewhere was suggested she would mess up the arrangements to such an extent that invariably the event was cancelled. So bad was her attitude that a very good male friend of hers said that she was using Ben, and always had.

Dina was an enigma and special in her own way. Her understanding of the situation between Ben and me made her seem almost saintly, but at the same time seemed almost unreal. She was vague and in many ways quite uncoordinated, particularly when it came to eating. Whoever had the misfortune to sit next to her whilst she ate, which was often, would invariably get sprayed with flying food. And as she would usually swing her legs to and fro at the same time the poor person would not only be covered in food but bruises as well. I learned this early on so tried hard always to make sure not to eat in her vicinity.

Her thin lips were plastered in shiny, red lipstick, usually crooked under her retroussé nose. Her glossy black hair was worn in a bob and her eyes were brown and vacant. Her legs were thin, her body large with a huge stomach and voluminous breasts and her bottom flat. Her hands and legs were always jerking.

She spent hours on the phone usually arguing with her friends, most of whom were male, and she didn't seem to have any conception at all of long or short distance calls. And when it came to her many men friends she freely admitted that they knew she only liked to be kissed here and there, touched a little bit but nothing more. They all apparently understood this. She said she had hardly ever experienced an orgasm and generally felt sexually inadequate.

She was terribly forgetful about many things. She would always be misplacing or losing her door keys. I once gave her a chain to put round her neck to keep her keys on but she lost that within a week. She used to leave taps on and on more than one occasion flooded not only her own flat but the one downstairs as well. She was always shocked and apologetic when told what she had done, but it didn't deter her from doing it again and again.

She needed handling with kid gloves most of the time and if upset, usually at the slightest thing, her moods could last for days, even weeks. Once in a mood she was impossible to deal with and best left alone.

If they invited people to their flat Ben would normally do the cooking and tell everyone that Dina had done it. If they were invited to someone else's house for a meal it was often a lottery. She would focus her conversations mostly on sex or the afterlife and then suddenly stop in mid sentence and say "will you excuse me if I lie down for a while a while, I'm quite sleepy. Have you a pillow and a blanket I could borrow?" Quite offputting!

She was a very strange mixture of being childish one minute and talking deeply and interestingly about the afterlife the next.

Borrowed lipsticks would be returned broken or badly squashed. Perfume bottles would be opened and spilt on a carpet. Ornaments would be dropped and broken. People who knew her just accepted that is what you got with Dina.

She was a user of people and didn't suffer fools gladly. She was a good flatterer if it was in her interests. People often would think her limited but I always knew her to be more cunning and clever than the impression she gave, particularly when it came to getting her own way. She would often give the impression to people that she was relaxed or accepting of a situation whilst inwardly she would be jealous. She would also often be very covetous of other people's things or belongings, what they were wearing or eating. Her attitude to what she called "Benny's love affair" with me was also interesting.

"I can see why Benny loves you. You give him what I can't. I also love you. You give me something as well. I think you are a rare and beautiful woman. I find most people boring but you are exciting and interesting. You seem to know what life is all about and I admire you. If it makes Benny happy, make love. Why not? I know he loves you very much. Some nights I hold him in my arms while he says he loves you and cries. I am not a possessive woman but I don't want a divorce. I need Benny for things. I can't work or find another man easily. Be with us, live with us. Then Benny will be happy. He will stop crying"

It was as if she was happy to lend me her husband but at the same time keep control of him, me and the situation. The three of us were out one evening for a meal when she noticed the watch I was wearing. A good one I might add. She held out her wrist and pointed to the one she was wearing. Ben had bought it for her and she was complaining. "Look what he buys me. A child's watch, not

103

a grown up's watch. It's an insult". We teased Ben about what he had done but both Ben and I knew why. She would only lose it or break it within a week. I asked her if she really did like mine and when she said she did I took it off, handed it to her and offered to swap it for hers. She agreed immediately and turning to Ben said "See how special she is. I can see why you love her so much". She then turned to me and said "You didn't have to give me your watch just because I let you sleep with my husband"

TWENTY

We all returned to England. It was cold and Ben still had no job. I was working for the same company as a medical rep and had a lot of time on my hands. Ben started to sell toys and I was able to help him. All Dina said was "Sell more toys, Benny, I want a new coat"

The situation was still difficult. Ben wanted to leave Dina but couldn't leave his children.

Christmas arrived and I bought Ben a lovely ring and then he was offered a job at the Connaught Hotel in Covent Garden. He took it but hated it. But at least we were in England, we both had jobs and we were madly in love. We were so happy when we were together and we met every day for lunch at Brahms and Liszt in Covent Garden.

Martin only had a short time left at school and when it was time Ben and I were going to be together. He was going to tell Dina that he was in love with me and wanted a divorce.

Dina had other ideas. She told him that if they ever divorced she would make sure he didn't have access to the children which made him extremely upset and afraid. She also stopped me going upstairs to their flat so Ben had to come to me for us to be together. As a result of all this everyone was unhappy. Ben was even speaking of having a six month trial with Dina for the sake of the children.

Then, out of the blue, a telegram arrived from the Rock Hotel in Eilat in Israel offering Ben a job. Eilat is on the Red Sea and enjoys, if that's the right word, a temperature of 44 degrees in the shade with a humidity of nine. Then it was a shabby shanty town lacking in culture cut off from the rest of the country. It was a far cry from

London and Covent Garden, the Brahms and Liszt, the Festival and Albert Halls, the theatres and Museums, the people and the restaurants. Everything that Ben and I loved. About the only thing it had going for it was its magical and mysterious atmosphere and it's uniquely strange, wild beauty. It was also the port where the Queen of Sheba arrived after crossing from Ethiopia to visit King Solomon. Ben had read the Songs of Solomon to me so many times that I was familiar with the stories.

Ben hated the idea of going but Dina said that if he didn't take the job this time she would divorce him and keep the children. We decided to go and find out more about the job and the place.. Ben left on one plane for Eilat and I followed on another. Once there at least we were together. Still desperately in love.

The job offered to Ben was the position of manager of the Hotel. One evening we were sitting and discussing the job in about the only decent restaurant in town called Mandy's, named after the owner Mandy Rice Davis. We talked and talked about the pros and cons of Eilat as against remaining in London. We decided that Ben would phone the Connaught Hotel in London to see if he still had the job there. If he did we would return to London. When he called he discovered that his job was no longer available so he reluctantly signed on the dotted line with the Rock and took the job.

We stayed in Eilat for a short holiday, enjoying a wonderful Friday "Shabbat" at the Laromme Hotel. We cried a lot, made passionate love a lot whilst we were there. I also found that Eilat was growing on me. There was something about it that created a strange attraction to me even though it lacked all the things I would miss. I loved the colours of the desert, the mountains, the sea. The feel of the warm air on my skin was very sensual. I felt I could write there and grow, so far from civilization, so close to the Bible. So close to God.

Our lovely holiday came to an end and it was time to return home, which we did reluctantly.

Back home with the family but the situation with Ben, and my job, was making me very unhappy. I started a new job as a medical rep but on the training course I couldn't concentrate, eat, sleep or work properly. As a result I was asked to leave. Ben was to leave soon and the days were flying by far too quickly. Ben had put the flat up for rent. We were both sick of love and despair. I thought I would die of heartbreak without him.

When the time came for him to leave he left me with the air fare to follow but he wanted the six month trial with Dina before I could join him. He left and I thought I would go out of my mind. I would wake at all times during the night, crying and in physical pain. I was shattered and confused and desperate for Ben. I wanted the life we'd had and now lost. I couldn't even look at the photo of him that he had left with me. After a few days he called me and told me he was just as sick as me. He said that he had put his mind into the job and his marriage. But he missed me terribly. "Come" he implored "I need you. Get your ticket and come to me. I need you, I'm dying without you!"

I was so desperate to go but at the same time afraid to do so. What if I went and then he wouldn't see me because of the trial with Dina. Friends who I spoke to about it said I should leave him and his family alone and let him try to make a go of things with Dina. I was distraught. I suffered and suffered until I felt completely burnt out. I felt totally lost and disillusioned. He said he loved me but at the same time said he wanted to make a go of things with Dina. How could it be so? I felt bereaved. One day I had a man to love and a man to love me. The next day, nothing. I felt totally alone with my tears and memories and fears.

I couldn't just let things go though. I decided I had to go to Eilat. I decided I would take a year off and write. It was now six weeks since Ben had left and I felt sick and weak. I had to do something. The children were all happy for me to go. They kept telling me that they hated seeing me so lifeless and depressed. I had bought a Honda fifty moped to ship out to Eilat and Martin had shown me how to start it. I practised with it in the bedroom.

My good friends Nora and Tony threw a farewell party for me and a number of my friends came along. They were all sad to see me go, they thought Ben should come for me and marry me.

I left the next day.

TWENTY ONE

It was 4 a.m. I had arrived in Eilat. It was hot.

I took a cab to the caravan that I had hired to live in temporarily, just by the sea, north of the city. I dumped my suitcases and called Ben at the Rock Hotel, where he was working. I was shaking as Ben said he was afraid I would unbalance him. I said I needed to see him and he agreed to come over the following morning. I put the phone down, lit a candle and sat and felt sick. I felt ugly and lifeless. And waited. Surely he would calm me and cure me. I was sure he would. And if I couldn't be with him, have a life together I would have to be strong and mend myself. I knew that if that was what had to be done I would have to extricate myself from him slowly. I knew I wouldn't be able to do it suddenly as I would probably never recover.

Ben came over at 10 o'clock in the morning. He looked so thin and we kissed and sat locked in each other's arms. We arranged to meet the next day and talk. He said he was working very hard but was so very pleased to see me. Seeing him I realized that I would heal and once again enjoy my life, even if I had to let him go and do it slowly.

The time in Eilat to start with seemed to take an eternity to pass but pass it did and I got into a routine that helped. I moved into a service apartment and I saw Ben for an hour most days. His work, and his commitment to Dina made it almost impossible to do anything else. My life started to form a pattern but I got tired of the situation. I started to feel aggressive towards Ben. I stopped making love with him, which made him upset, when I really began to realize that he would never leave Dina. I became jealous of the fact that he seemed to have everything whilst I felt so

109

alone, waiting for him to visit. I knew I had to do something.

I had visits from both Norman and from Sara. They both stayed at Ben's hotel and were made welcome. As I was whenever I visited. Dina was happy to see me and it was OK for me to visit Ben at the hotel whenever I wanted. I spent time at the pool or the beach and even Friday nights were spent with Ben and Dina and their family, but only at the hotel, not at their apartment. I seemed to lack nothing except the knowledge that Ben and I would never be together as I wanted. He seemed to be a happy man again feeling that he had both Dina and me, and his children.

My service apartment was expensive and although Ben offered to pay for it I didn't want him to so found a small, seedy flat overlooking Aquaba. Sara came to look at it with me and loved it. She thought it could be made to look very lovely. I moved as soon as Sara had returned to England and soon loved it. I became content with my life. I had the sun, wine, candlelight, Ben and no responsibilities. I felt that for the first time in my life I was living for just me. Although there were times when I felt lonely I was determined to gain from the experience, to find out what and who I really was. As it got dark each night I would sit on my balcony with a glass or two of wine and look at the lights of Aquaba. I slowly strengthened both my body and my soul.

Six months after I had moved to my flat Martin finished school and came to live with me. It was wonderful to have him with me. We drank wine and talked of his future, the only problem being neither of us was too sure what his future entailed. He didn't know what he really wanted to do so we agreed that whilst he was with me we would treat the time as a breathing space with no pressure on him. Ben gave him a job as a bellboy at the hotel with the words " A PhD you won't get Martin, but you will earn some cash and who knows you might get laid!" This was said mainly because Martin was always bemoaning to me and Ben that he was still a virgin and was desperate "to do it". He said he was probably the only boy at his school who hadn't.

Suddenly I was offered a job as a courier for a travel company which operated in London. Why not, I thought. I had made friends in Eilat and on my birthday I borrowed a friend's garden to host a party to celebrate. As I looked round at the guests I realized that in many ways I had gone full circle. The people with me were so similar to the friends I had made in London. Professional, successful people with interests similar to my own. The local doctor and the local dentist and their wives; an artist and a famous theatre producer. A lawyer and his wife. Good friends who have remained so to this day. I had made a life beyond Ben.

One evening Martin returned home, after a date with a woman ten years his senior, beaming from ear to ear. "I've done it, Mum. She let me do it". I got out the Brandy, a celebration was in order and we toasted his right of passage to "manhood". Martin called Ben to tell him. As a result Ben arranged a small party with Martin as guest of honour. Dina, smiling, asked "How was it, Mart?"

My job was fun and I was meeting lots of interesting people. I was allowed to breakfast in any of the local hotels and I made the most of it. My life was beautiful. I was even enjoying driving round the town on my little moped, albeit a little erratically. The locals were all very careful when I was around, calling me "the mad

Englishwoman". I would wobble dangerously to work each morning and then repeat the exercise in the opposite direction on the way home in the evening. I eventually decided to stop with the motor bike for two reasons. One, I fell off several times. The second was Martin saying "Mum, when do you think you will grow up?"

I was enjoying the job. The people I worked with, Jean and Bruce, were very nice and easy to work with. Bruce was from London and Jean, a spinster of forty three, whilst as bossy as hell, became a very good friend. I was also entitled to free flights home and at the end of the season Martin and I left Eilat. Martin had got a job in London and was going to be staying with Nora and Tony. I was going to take a break and spend some time catching up with my friends.

One day I got a call from Ben, who was upset because it was now seven weeks since I had left Eilat and he was missing me. He said if I would go to Brahms and Liszt on Friday at noon there would be a surprise there for me. I had no idea what it could be and he wouldn't give me a clue. So on Friday I duly went along to Covent Garden and when I got to the restaurant there was my surprise. It was Ben. It was so wonderful to see him, to be with him. We spent a whole week together and it was, in many ways, just like it had been. Because of the smallness of Eilat and our full lives there our life together had been non existent but here in London we had the space and the time to enjoy each other again. But soon, too soon, it was time for Ben to return home to Dina. We both cried.

I eventually returned to Eilat but virtually as soon as I got there I was offered the chance of working in Tel Aviv. By this time I had also bought a little red VW beetle which

112

I christened Petal. I thought it would be a good idea to try Tel Aviv and Ben helped me load up Petal and travel there. Once I had settled in Ben used to come over twice a week and we would dine in some beautiful restaurant and then make love before he flew back home. Whilst it was great to see him and spend time with him the situation was still upsetting. He would never tell me if he was staying or not until the evening was virtually over. He would send me flowers but I would invariably throw them out of the window in a fit of pique.

On top of the unsatisfactory Ben situation Tel Aviv was a mistake. I was lonely, I missed my friends and my life in Eilat. I missed my little flat. I missed Jean. I was going through a bad period again. My life was becoming a burden again.

Norman called to say that he wanted to see me with a possibility of rekindling our relationship. Ben said he thought it was a good idea, as did Jean. Norman visited me and was very sweet and attentive. We stayed as guests at Bens hotel for a short stay and then we returned to London to try again.

My flat in London was fortunately empty so I moved back in. That was about the only good news for a while. The "thing" with Norman didn't work and we split up. Ben kept calling to say he missed me terribly. It was cold in London, certainly a lot colder than I was used to. My car and my life were back in Israel. The one good thing was that the children were all busy and happy. Sara and Martin, although both had their own place, would often come and stay with me.

I had also renewed my friendship with Miles, the man who I had worked with in London as medical reps. We hadn't seen each other for a number of years but it was nice to see him again and we seemed to naturally to fit back into our friendship. Although we had never been lovers our relationship was close and personal. We would talk to each other intimately and at length about our fears, our hopes, our lives. When we had worked together so long ago we had often talked about being free from the work we hated and to live a relaxed life somewhere warm. To me it had, and still was, a reality but I always felt that to Miles it was just a dream. Something for him to talk about, not do. Coming back now it was great to see him but I was appalled to hear that he had a virus in the brain. He really wasn't well at all and I was shocked to see how wasted away he was. When we had first met a few years ago he had been a fat and jolly man, full of fun. Now he was thin, distant and seemingly drifting away from reality and life.

One day we had breakfast and agreed to meet soon for dinner but he died before we could do so. I missed him terribly and felt angry at the waste of a life. I wondered if he had come to join me in the sun whether his life may have been prolonged. His funeral, a few days later, was terrible for me. There were not too many people there and those that were seemed old. I wondered if that had been all he had gathered in his life and it made me very sad.

I sold my flat and Pembar Avenue and was free, once again, to return to Eilat.

TWENTY TWO

At last I was back in Eilat, feeling both elated and sad. I contemplated my life and what I had been through and what I needed. I was cured of Ben at long last, mainly due to his own lack of care and consideration for me. I would sit and face my beloved gulf but lacked the incentive to work or study. I missed having a close relationship, feeling that it was important for me to enjoy one to function. Perhaps I would start a new chapter in my life. And then I did.

One lunchtime I was sitting in a local hotel, alone, when a man sat down opposite me. I didn't want to be bothered by conversation and tried to ignore him. My mind was too occupied with my need to find a flat. About fortyish, he spoke with a very pleasant voice and an American accent and said hello. I tried to ignore him but as he seemed very pleasant and polite I relented and we started to talk. He asked me about myself and what I was doing. I told him of my need to find a flat. At this he seemed to get quite animated and said that he was as well and would I consider flat sharing with him. I studied him, wondering about his motives, but he seemed intelligent, well spoken and pleasant. I made a quick decision and said yes. We agreed that we would start looking together for a suitable flat.

That evening I met a male friend for dinner. He worked in the desert but lived in America. I knew he was keen on me but was not too sure if I felt the same about him. We had a very enjoyable evening and he even mentioned that he was considering renting a villa by the sea and wanted me to live there with him. I told him I would think about it but didn't tell him about my potential "flat sharing" arrangement.

The following evening I was to meet a female friend for dinner but she didn't show up. As I was waiting for her who should show up but my potential flatmate. I told him that my dinner date hadn't shown and he immediately invited me to his place to eat. He said he was very good at salads. As we were likely to be flatmates I thought it would be a good idea to get to know him, even though in the back of my mind I knew there was also the offer to live by the sea with my other friend.

We had a nice dinner, after which we went to a nearby bar to have a drink and to dance. Not only had he been an excellent salad maker, as he had boasted, but he also turned out to be an excellent dancer as well. We had a lovely evening and I felt myself warming towards him. We returned home and made love rather shyly. After he was considerate and attentive, asking me if I felt comfortable and I said I did. It had been a very enjoyable evening.

A few night later I was having dinner with the male friend who had offered me the chance to live by the sea with him and I was on the verge of saying yes. As I sat there I suddenly caught sight of the "flatmate" outside. He looked really lonely and I pulled the curtain down so that he wouldn't see me. I felt quite treacherous to him but as I raised a glass to toast him in my mind it helped me make a decision. I felt good about things for the rest of the evening and then I told my companion that I wouldn't be joining him by the sea. He was very angry but I didn't seem to care.

The very next day I phoned the "flatmate" and told him about a flat I had seen with a balcony and a wonderful view of Aquaba. He wanted to see it. A few days later we signed a six month contract and moved in together.

Our life together was, for the most part, good. I shopped, cooked, cleaned and worked. He made me laugh and made me angry in equal measure. We made love, which I have to say was initially disappointing. His children came to stay, as did mine. We had many friends and many thoroughly enjoyable dinner parties with them. And our love making gradually became more wild, more expressive, more enjoyable. But at the same time I was worried. Whilst I felt I was falling in love he seemed unable to commit saying things like "but you are just my flatmate". It was a strange relationship because it seemed that neither of us really knew what we were to each other or what we really wanted from our togetherness. We were loyal and supportive to each other and I was happy in that he allowed me my freedom. But whilst he appeared confident I saw that he was, in fact quite negative and unsure in many ways. What bought it home to me was our "adventure" with Bunty Moon!

Bunty Moon was a small tortoise shell kitten which I got for my flatmate. She was small, round, very sweet and fell in love with him as soon as they met. She made a fuss of him, far more than she did with me, and he spoilt her. Then one day the kitten went out and didn't come back. Two or three days passed and still no sign of Bunty Moon. Flatmate was extremely upset so I got him another cat, this time a small grey one. But this time they didn't get on at all and that seemed to make matters worse. I prayed to St Anthony, the saint I always prayed to, to help me find things, usually successfully. The very following day there was a mewing at the door and opening it we were amazed to see Bunty Moon standing there. We were overjoyed but not for long. The cat seemed to have changed. She was now more wild and bad tempered, and didn't seem to like my flatmate anymore. She had changed completely. I returned the grey cat. My flatmate declared that it couldn't be Bunty Moon, that it was a different cat. I couldn't work out if it was Bunty Moon or not. He changed from being quite negative about the new cat to being more positive and told me to get rid of it. He didn't want it. That evening I took it to the hotel where I worked and left it there. A little after I had returned home there was another mewing at the door. Opening it I was amazed to see the cat. I assumed it had followed me home but as it came in it made a beeline for my flatmate and nuzzled against his legs. This time it really was our Bunty Moon and we couldn't believe that we had even considered the "lookalike" cat to be her. I thought that perhaps St Anthony had been a little drunk when I prayed to him and thought he would help me out by sending a cat that just looked like Bunty Moon. Not very helpful. But we were delighted to get the real Bunty Moon back and I realized that my flatmate was only really positive when something mattered to him. The experience seemed to change something in me and in the relationship.

I had told my flatmate about Ben and how much I had loved him but he was married and about our three year affair but that it was over. We would often see Ben at his hotel where we went for drinks. The two men had even become friends. I even told him about Norman and the difficult relationship I had with him. I said that I had ended the relationship some time ago but that Norman had never quite accepted it. Norman even phoned me to say that he still loved me and was coming to see me to rekindle our relationship. I told him I didn't want him to and that I was happy with my flatmate. Norman said he was coming anyway.

That New Years Eve Ben had invited us to the hotel to celebrate but it didn't end happily. As I sat at the table and looked round I felt how ironic life could be .At the table was my son; Ben, my ex lover; another ex lover, Norman; and my current lover, the flatmate. Talk about past, present and future!

I told my flatmate about what I thought and felt but instead of being understanding or sympathetic he told me he didn't like what he called my attitude. I certainly didn't like his and we quarrelled bitterly then left the party. After that he would often make sarcastic comments about my "irony of life" and made it clear that he no longer liked me. I felt we had lost something important in our relationship and that it was unlikely to be regained.

I desperately needed to make some firm decisions about my life and where I was going. One evening as I sat on the balcony of my flat with Sara I made up my mind.

As we sat I was acutely aware of the sounds and smells and feelings of living in Israel. I could hear the Arabic music drifting from a nearby flat, I could see a pregnant woman in another lumbering from room to room. A man doing his ironing in yet another. Car horns hooting, men shouting greetings to each other on the streets below. The smells of a spicy dish being prepared somewhere close to hand. Sara and I were lethargic and discussing the future. I told her of my decisions. I had decided to take a job as a Public Relations officer at the Caravan Hotel. Ben and Dina were relocating to Jerusalem the following week and the six month agreement on the flat was coming to an end . As was the relationship with my flatmate.

I told Sara that I was also going to buy a small house in the desert.

TWENTY THREE

After seeing quite a few houses I decided on one that was out of town and facing the mountains. It needed a few changes as I had decided to run it as a Bed & Breakfast. My ex-flatmate agreed to help me and to find the best workmen for the job and then took a months vacation to oversee everything. The house was finished, my furniture arrived from England and I was in business. I knew the bed & breakfast would do well and I was looking forward to everything. I felt free and knew I could live alone again which made me feel strong. I had Fanny, my little dog, for company, ex-flatmate would occasionally drop round for a meal and even Ben, my ex lover, called a few times a week. People began arriving to stay, I started writing and life seemed full of promise. I was happy.

And then my life changed. I was having dinner with my friend Jean, and her new husband, in their home, when a friend of theirs appeared. He was very tall, 6'4" I discovered later, and had to stoop to enter. A large man with unruly brown hair, a droopy moustache, heavy framed glasses and brown smooth arms. Impressive, I thought, a man with style. He was a good conversationalist and the evening was enjoyable. When it was time to leave he and I left together, went for a drink and continued talking into the small hours.

Mike, that was his name. was an American working in the Negev Desert, North of Eilat, helping to build an airbase. He told me that most of his working life had been spent overseas, at one point spending eight years in Bangkok. I told him of my need to get off the treadmill of life and find myself, and how I was doing just that in Israel.

He appreciated my way of thinking and wanted to see me again. He was interesting and interested, a man of the world and extremely charming. A true gentleman. I didn't want to get too close to another man just yet. I had experienced my big love and I was happy with that. Mike, I felt, viewed things differently. He wanted and needed to be involved. He'd been alone for over a year and had another two years in the job he was doing. I agreed to see him, we arranged a meeting and then I drove home.

Eilat was experiencing extremely hot weather at the time and it had been 115 degrees during the day but now as I drove to my house on the edge of the desert the air was cool and pleasant. I could see the inviting lights of Aquaba on the far side of the Red Sea twinkling and it made me reflect on my life and the place I had chosen as my refuge.

Eilat was south of the Red Sea and just 5 kilometers north of what had been Israel but was now Egypt. After the six day war seven years previously the territory had been under Israel's governance but the peace talks between Sadat of Egypt and Begin of Israel had resulted in it being returned to Egypt. Eilat itself , as a city, was particularly uninspiring and unstimulating having just one cinema, a poorly filled department store, a few dirty fruit and vegetable shops, a supermarket and a couple of overpriced restaurants.

What it did have however was a charm and a presence that was quite magical. The surrounding mountains reflecting in the Red Sea with their constantly changing colours created a fantastically ethereal beauty which, combining with the hot sensual, desert wind really claimed ones senses. And the constant stream of the Bedouin and their camels along the desert beaches are truly colourful accompaniments to an already colourful and mind blowing landscape.

The timeless charm of Eilat.

FRIENDS IN HIGH - AND LOW - PLACES.

Before continuing the story of my life and times in Eilat I thought it would be an interesting diversion to introduce some of the friends I had made in my time there.

I was enjoying my life as a courier for the English travel agent and I had a wide selection of colleagues, contacts, acquaintances and close friends.

Jean was a work colleague and she and I became good friends even though she had a tendency to be rather bossy. Single at the time, she lived in a run down, crummy apartment and tended to use orange boxes for furniture. Due to the jobs we did she and I would often be invited to restaurants for free meals or offered "complimentary" trips on the many yachts which plied their trade on the Red Sea. We made the most of the quality of life these "adventures" offered and had a lot of fun together.

Yolande and Etty were both painters and both interesting. Yolande was a committed feminist and all her paintings were of women in servitude. Her husband, Michyael, was a dentist and had a remarkable likeness to Yves Montand, a popular French film star of the time. Or so we liked to think. Etty, a Morrocan Israeli, was a rather large lady who, it seemed to me, just got larger and larger as our friendship progressed. Her paintings were particularly good and she was very artistic. She even persuaded me to pose nude for the art classes a couple of nights a week, which made me a little extra cash. Her husband was Ben who was Belgian and a mad extrovert and could talk ten languages. A diver in the Israeli army he would often disappear on secret missions.

The two friends who were particularly interesting for me were Kay and Celia, whose lives were far from dull.

KAY

Known as Plain Kay she and her husband Ronald had emigrated to Israel twenty years previously from Birmingham. Ronald, a very military looking gentleman, was a doctor who had been struck off the English register but practiced in Eilat. He liked to refer to himself as the highly qualified "London Doctor". He was always immaculately dressed and spoke to all and sundry in an assertive booming voice. His patients all tended to receive the same treatment, whatever their ailment. A jab. The difference was that males received theirs in the arm whilst the female patients received theirs in the rump. The other difference being that males were charged cash, the females could give "a kiss and a squiggly cuddle". As most of his patients were female and young his income was low. He was a terrible doctor. It was a standing joke that whilst Ronald had never killed anyone he had never cured anyone either as most people when they were ill took themselves to the hospital rather than consult him.

But back to Kay. She was able to put up with Ronald and his "ways" because of her other life. Plain, middle aged and busy she seemed to involve herself in everyone else's problems and affairs, offering help and advice in varying degrees. As there was much wife beating and many affairs in the town Kay was kept very busy.

Her approach to housework was also somewhat iconic inasmuch as she kept her house as messy, dirty and untidy as was possible to just function. Not helped by the fact that she had a habit of taking in all kinds of stray

125

animals. Her unconventionality and her appearance led most people to consider her both undesirable and, in turn, lacking in desire. Nothing was further from the truth. She was full of desires and was desperate to be desired. To her it didn't matter if the person to answer her needs was male or female, she was bi-sexual. She knew what she wanted but at the same time did not want to jeopardise her life as the "doctor's wife". She knew that what she was looking for would be secret and was confident she would find it. She was also patient.

About once a month Kay would journey to Tel Aviv, stay overnight and deal with commitments she had through the various self-organised, self-named and self-run committees she was on. On one of her visits she learned of a club in the North of the city which seemed worth a visit. The only problem was it was in the Arab quarter and was the area where prostitutes, gays and transvestites gathered. Not, therefore. a safe place for a single woman, even a plain one like Kay, to venture alone. But Kay had an answer. Whenever there had been a fancy dress party in Eilat, and there were quite a few, Kay would transform herself into dashing, if somewhat camp, male. She would sleek back her short curly hair, make up her face very carefully with arched, black eyebrows, don male clothing. This, she decided would be her way of getting to the club. A club where, she hoped, she would find the answer to a dreary life and an overbearing husband. A club in which she might find the love and affection that was lacking in her life.

At the bar she decided to order a large scotch on the rocks, rather than the boring sherry she would normally drink at home. As she twirled the drink in her mouth the hot shock seemed to travel through her whole body, even down to her feet. She looked round at the assorted clientele and noticed a very pretty, but very large, woman across the room. She was immediately attracted to her and wanted her. She thought to herself "One more of these and I'll approach the big lady. I'll have a night to enjoy, doing my own thing, and tomorrow go back to being Plain Kay with the kids and the unsatisfactory life."

The "big lady" turned out to be Phoebe, who'd been a member of the club for two years, and lived in Ramatgan, two miles from Tel Aviv. Married at sixteen to a man she now called "the egotist" she had accumulated seven children and was now still only 32. Her husband beat her regularly. He'd even attacked the kids and the police had been called on more than one occasion. Although nearly two hundred pounds Phoebe was still a very vivacious and attractive woman. She'd had a lesbian lover for some time but the lover had met an American man who was now fulfilling all her sexual needs. So much so that she had transferred to the "straight" life. That had been six months previously and Phoebe was still trying to get over the trauma. She'd contemplated suicide but didn't feel she could leave her children in the hands of the "egotist".

She had also noticed Kay as she had entered the club and the attraction was mutual. She thought Kay looked "a commanding and confident dyke", not the sort to run off with the first man who offered her a fuck.

CELIA

Before coming to Eilat, where I met her, Celia had lived in an attic flat in an old house in the Archway Road,

127

London. *Financially she was doing well, it was everything else that seemed, to her, to be crap. Although her attic flat was convenient inasmuch that she was away from the constant traffic noise and there was no one above her to disturb her life her constant thought was "I want my own bathroom". She hated having to share with the other tenants.*

Celia was a croupier at one of the Park Lane casinos and this was where she was able to earn good money. Twenty nine and divorced (but made a widow just before the divorce finalised) she'd had various lovers but only one relationship which had meant anything or lasted. That had been with John but he had finished it when he became fed up with her constant self-pity and preoccupation with herself. Celia, being an honest person, accepted he had a reason. "I know I'm a bore and a failure" she would say "I don't get on with people, they don't like me, I'm not friendly enough". She was very worried about losing her job (she was "boring and unfriendly") because she felt unsure what else she could do. She'd previously been a croupier on a cruise ship but had lost the job by sleeping with all the crew and staff. She admitted that she wouldn't have slept around so much if one of them had stayed around for a while, rather than just one night. She'd look at herself in the mirror and knew she was looking at a pretty girl with a good figure, good breasts, a slim waist, good legs. She had a lot to offer but no one was buying.

Even her current relationship, with Alan, was a disaster. He was 21, into drugs and unemployed when what she really longed for was a person who would love her, look after her, provide her with a home – "with an unshared bathroom"

She had a two week holiday coming up and felt she really needed to get away and try and sort her life out. Whilst deciding what to do and where to go she noticed an article in The Sunday Times all about Eilat. Sun, sand, easy direct flights from Gatwick, cheap accommodation deals. She booked.

On arriving in Eilat she was met at her hotel and shown to her room, insisting on checking before she signed in that it had its own bathroom. It did and she settled in, the courier promising to call the next day with details of local tours, restaurants, clubs, places of interests etc. Celia booked trips to see Solomon's Pillars in Jerusalem and the Canyon of Inscriptions during her second week, deciding that in the first week she would amuse herself with the tall, good looking, sexy Israeli who ran the bar next door to the hotel – plus a few other men who had taken her eye. "What's the harm" she said to herself "I'm leaving in two weeks. I can sleep with them all if I want" She did. She had a great time. Not being able to speak Hebrew and getting by with pidgin English they didn't know if she was boring. Even if they did they wouldn't have cared, she was just "another tourist".

The trip to Jerusalem took place on the Tuesday of the second week and she was picked up at five in the morning for the four hour trip through the Negev Desert. The driver/guide explained to the group of twenty tourists that he would show them the old city, the Ville Delorosa, the stations of the cross and then stop for dinner at a good Jerusalem restaurant. They would stay at the American Colony Hotel, then on to Bethlehem, returning to Eilat the following evening. Celia liked the idea of the trip but also decided she liked the look of the blond Israeli guide even more.

On the journey she chatted with him and by the time they reached the Judean Hills they both knew, without saying anything, that they would be spending the night together. He spoke fluent English (later she was to find out he also spoke another seven languages quite fluently as well) and was very good looking. She discovered that he was 33, owned his own apartment in Eilat, he wasn't married, he ran a Mercedes and had a half share in a boat. He'd returned to Israel a month previously after spending five years in Brazil and was now looking for a wife.

They started an affair and as she only had three days left of her holiday it started at quite a pace and developed quickly.

She discussed the possibility of staying on longer with the courier. She agreed that as she didn't have much to lose in London she would extend her holiday for a month and see how things went.

She moved in with Dan into what turned out to be a rather seedy little flat and after her months extension was up they decided she would return to London, finish with her flat, pack her belongings in her old Triumph and drive across Europe into Haifa and on to Eilat.

On her return to Eilat she married Dan and commenced complaining almost immediately about the weather, the people, the flat, the food, the TV. In fact she complained about just about everything – especially Dan. She said she hated everything and was better off in London. So much so that people started to get rather fed up and bored by her constant harping. The courier, who quickly

130

lost patience with her, suggested she would be better off in London and should return there. After much crying and to-ing and fro-ing she did actually go to London. As soon as she got there she discovered she was pregnant so returned to Dan in Eilat. She stayed nine months, complaining all the time, gave birth to a boy and then returned to England to live with her parents. Her pathological complaining, however, didn't stop. So much so that her father got totally exasperated and told her to go back to Dan. She did.

Her complaining just didn't stop and she continued to hate everything. At least she was honest enough to admit it was all her fault. She was determined to leave Dan for good and as far as I know she is still complaining about everything.

TWENTY FOUR

Sara came to Eilat for a holiday and I introduced her to Mike and asked her what she thought I should do. I told her I liked him a lot but didn't want to completely lose my independence. Sara liked him and her advice to me, before returning to London, was to relax into the relationship as she felt it could be a good one.

The day she left Mike and I made wild and uninhibited love in the garden even though I instinctively knew my hard earned independence was in danger. Mike was warm and sweet and our relationship blossomed. He invited me to go on a short vacation with him but I was worried about leaving the bed and breakfast so I delayed giving him an answer.

And then I got the phone call that changed everything.

It was from my friend Tony in London and it was to tell me that Sara was badly ill. She had a malignant melanoma. He said I should return immediately as Sara was due an operation at the Westminster Hospital. I was horrified. The phone shook in my hand. I had so many questions and didn't know where to start. How bad was it? What was the prognosis? How was Sara? Would she live? Tony told me to book a flight as soon as possible, let them know when and Nora, his wife, would meet me at the airport. I put the phone down sat down and shook uncontrollably. I needed to phone Ashley in Australia. I had no idea what the time was there and still shaking and crying dialled his number. I thought I'd misdialled as nothing happened and I replaced the phone in its cradle. Just then the phone rang. It was Ashley. I thought it was in response to my call but it wasn't, it was sheer coincidence. He was on holiday in Hong Kong and was just phoning me to say hello. I told him about Sara and how scared I was. "We need you. Come home" I implored. We agreed that he would call England to speak to Tony to find out what he could. He did so and called me back. "It is serious" he said "I'll come home immediately. They will delay the operation until we are there". He was crying as he spoke.

I called Mike and he came from the desert and spent the whole night holding me in his arms while I cried. He gave me the money for the flight and everything was arranged for my return. Mike was a true friend.

I bought a gold chain at the airport for Sara to bring her luck. The flight was delayed and I think I must have cried all the way home. Nora was at the airport and we drove straight to the hospital. She told me that Ashley had arrived and was waiting for us there.

When we arrived at the hospital I rushed to see Sara. She was a mix of fear and bravery and we sat and talked and talked. She said the operation was to be the next morning. When it was time to leave I found it almost impossible to leave her but I did and went home with Ashley. We were up all night crying and praying and the following day found it extremely difficult to fill the time before we could go to the hospital. I think it was just more crying and praying most of the time. I was petrified of losing Sara. How could I ever face life without her.

We eventually went to the hospital to see the surgeon who had operated on her. "It's in the bucket" were the words he started the conversation with. "It was caught in time and Sara now has the same chance as all of us. We'll keep an eye on her regularly for about five years but as far as we can tell she has a fresh start" Our prayers had obviously worked. I gave a large thanks to God.

Sara had recovered from the operation and was sitting up in bed, smiling and looking beautiful. Her boyfriend Bill was with her.

Sara's positive mind helped the start of her recovery and after a week Ashley returned to Australia. Sara was in the hospital for ten days and after she came out I stayed for about a week before I returned to Eilat. A week or so after that she and Bill came for a holiday in the sun.

The experience changed me irrevocably. Ever since I have lived with the fear inside me not just for Sara but for everyone I love.

TWENTY FIVE

I returned to the desert but felt drained, incredibly heavy and sad. I realized that it was lifes experiences that aged you not necessarily the passage of time. It was life itself that was the breaker of backs, the creator of furrows on the face and the deadness in the eyes. Laughter and joy make their own mark but it is temporary whereas the sorrows and troubles life create are more permanent. I felt my life was changing, but worse still I felt the change was beyond my control.

As I sat in the winter sun, smoking a cigar, I wept, realizing that things were changing. This was to have been my haven, far away from the negatives of my life, but I felt that the real world would soon be back and my peace would be at an end. Luckily I had Mike in my life and he gave me strength.

He had asked me to join him on a holiday to Cyprus and even though I loved Cyprus, having been there many times, and wanted to go I had doubts. Mike was a strength to me and I knew if I went our relationship would develop but I was still a little unsure whether I wanted another close relationship. I thought of the independence I would lose, the income from the Bed & Breakfast I would miss, the new life I was creating I would have to give up.

I decided I would go and Mike was happy. He booked the holiday which was to be in three weeks. Whilst I waited for the holiday I spent time with the people I had staying in the B & B. They were a friendly, but mixed, bunch. I had two journalists, one from The Times, the other from The Jewish Chronicle; a lady called Poppy from Edinburgh who had been an orchestral musician; and two

135

boring "old Farts", a seventy year old man who moaned about everything and a woman in her mid forties, who followed me about all over the place. Mixed but interesting.

A few days before the trip Mike came over for dinner and as he was leaving we went into the garden and made love. It was spectacular and I seemed totally engulfed by his lovemaking. Mike was an extremely good and attentive lover, and I knew my feelings for him were growing.

The holiday seemed to me to be a mix of emotions. Mike and I found we were well suited to each other, in many ways, but I was not good company. I seemed to carry the burden of Sara's illness with me still. Mike was understanding and gave me "space".

On our return our relationship continued to grow apace. Physically and emotionally we got closer and closer. He would travel the hour and a half from the air base where he worked, spend the night with me and then get up at 3.45am for the return trip on the bus to work. He probably did this five nights a week, always bringing with him a red bag full of "goodies". Lobster, steak, oysters, shrimp and the very best French champagne. Mike supplied the very best food and wines, I tried to supply the very best ambience of elegance and love. The combination seemed to work very well.

We lived well and happily in our "oasis" with Fanny, my little dog and very few friends. We had each other. Mike, due to work and the long hours of travel, was often very tired and I tried to make few demands on him. On his days of I would enjoy taking a huge cooked breakfast for him to enjoy in bed. He would jokingly put in his "order"

"Could I please have hot chocolate, six pieces of French toast with butter and honey and jam, some bacon, four slices please, three glasses of orange juice. Oh and don't forget the ketchup". My smiling response would be a happy "Yes, Mike".

Mike, after a period of time, suggested I close down the bed & breakfast.

"I'm living with you, let's open up the house and forget the B&B. It'll be more private and comfortable for us."

"But, Mike, I need the income and the independence it gives me. And the interest. I'd miss the people"

Mike continued to press me to close it down. He said he would be more than happy to pay the bills and wanted to look after me. He said it would make sense. I told him I would think about it and let him know what I had decided in a few days.

The next day I sat down with Fanny the Dog and asked her what she thought about it all. Fanny was a desert coloured, rough looking small dog with green eyes. She was also my confidante and chief adviser! Fanny wagged her tail, licked me and said "Why not give it a twirl?" I agreed and told her I would tell Mike when he came next that I would close the B&B. "Good" said Fanny "I never did like those guests"

FANNY'S FOOD FETISH

Another slight digression as I tell you about Fanny's odd food fetish. And how it probably saved my life.

Fanny's favourite food was onion. Not just onion, but raw onion. The fact it was also one of mine was neither here nor there.

Her next favourite was caramel. I very rarely let her have caramel however, It wasn't very good for her and as I said to her "Caramel is bad for you and for your teeth and your figure. You want to stay beautiful, don't you?" Fanny, in fact was anything but beautiful, but as I told her often enough that she was she had grown to believe it.

But back to the onions.

On Mondays Mike would often not come over and this gave me and Fanny the opportunity to indulge in our passion. Raw onion.

I knew that chewing raw onion was not necessarily a help in a relationship and was therefore quite happy for Mike's absence on Mondays. I could indulge myself, as could Fanny, and this would invariably keep me going until the following Monday.

On this particular Monday Fanny had finished her raw onion allowance and was curled up fast asleep on the floor by my feet. I was still enjoying my allowance and was just raising a particularly delicious raw onion to my mouth when I heard a strange noise just outside the house. A lot of my friends thought my house was on the "wrong" side of town, and were always somewhat concerned by the collection of odd down and outs who often slept rough on a patch of waste land just outside my front gate. I wasn't normally too worried about them but the noise I heard *worried me. I went cold, even though the temperature must have been over 100 degrees. I called Fanny but she was beyond hearing, or caring, deep in her onion induced sleep. I heard another noise, this time inside the high, outer wall of the property, just the other side of the front door. I sat stock still, raw onion in hand, staring at the door, my heart pounding. The door slowly swung open to reveal a tall, dark man dressed in a caftan. I was transfixed with fear as he slowly approached me, his intentions clear and menacing as he revealed himself to me. He came closer and closer until I could feel his breath on my face. It was then the onions came into play. I breathed out the onion fumes straight into his leering face. He was obviously taken off guard by the unexpectedly foul smell and hesitated. In that split second I managed to pick up a mallet I had used earlier to hang a painting and had, fortunately, left out. I swung it as hard as I could and knocked him cold.*

Just then I heard more footsteps on the gravel as they approached the house. I stood facing the door, mallet in one hand, onion in the other. Mike walked in.

Even though it was a Monday and he shouldn't have been there I was mightily glad he was.

I cannot remember whether I finished my onion or not.

.

TWENTY SIX

A little after the famous raw onion night I got myself a small, low paying job, meeting tourists at the local airport and arranging local trips for any of them who were interested. If they were I would arrange to meet them at their hotel at an agreed time and day. I was happy to get the job because it gave me some personal pride to be working. It also gave me some money of my own. Mike was generous and liked to look after me but I needed my own self earned "pocket" money. With it I was able to buy Mike the odd little present or take him for a meal at the local Chinese restaurant.

Although at the start of my job I was sometimes a little "lost", both in direction and in knowledge of the local sites I was lucky inasmuch the tourists knew less than me. But it seemed to work and the tourists seemed to like my company as I drove them round in my little bashed and scratched bright red Beetle. And as the job went on I got more knowledgeable and confident. But, like a lot of good things, it came to an end. The weather was getting too hot for tourists and they ceased coming so my desert trips had to end.

Round about the time the job stopped Mike was asked to go to Tel Aviv for a month or so with his work. I decided to go with him, placed Fanny with a friend who would look after her and journeyed north. We stayed in a hotel and were able to meet for lunch every day. It was blissful and we had a great time. Mike's hours were really good, no more getting up at 3.45 as he would need to do back home in Eilat, and we enjoyed our time, filling it with so many things to do. I particularly like our trips to

Jerusalem and cocktails at the King David Hotel whilst we were there.

New Year's Eve, 1981, midnight in Tel Aviv. Mike and I kissed. I had a lovely feeling in knowing that I was in a "right" relationship and we were both looking forward to what we knew would be a good year.

The only thing that was wrong was my adventure in hair dyeing. I had told my friend Jean that I had made a decision to go blonde. She was appalled. "Don't be ridiculous" was her response. "You are too dark. It won't suit you"

I told her I was determined and even when she suggested I had blonde highlights to test my plan I insisted that I wanted to go completely blonde. Jean was convinced I was mad. Looking back I think she was right.

The appointment came, my hair was dyed. And the horror began.

My hair, instead of going blonde became a shitty, green colour. Even worse it started to break off in uneven clumps. I couldn't sleep and vomited most of the night between attempts at re-dying what was left of my hair back to its original black. When Mike turned up the following evening and saw my rather pitiful looking head he turned almost the same green as my hair had done. I hated the short hair that was left and although Mike was very sympathetic and suggested it would all be back to normal in a few weeks I knew it would need to be cut off right back to the roots.

I hated my looks and felt so ugly. I hated myself and the fact I looked like a member of the Harikrishna sect. It was awful. Wigs were no help as to my mind they always just looked like wigs. And it was too hot to wear them.

My only consolation as I faced the two years I knew it would take to grow out was I did have a well shaped skull.

TWENTY SEVEN

Mike and I made plans for a trip to the Far East. Mike left for Bangkok whilst I stayed on in Eilat for a week as Ashley and his new wife, Charlotte, were coming to stay with me. We had a most blissful week together but it was soon over and time for me to go and join Mike.

Ashley and Charlotte flew to Jerusalem and I flew to Athens, where I spent a day on my own to rest and relax before taking the flight to Bangkok later the same night. I enjoyed my day, particularly the solitary dinner with a bottle of Arsinoe, my favourite Greek wine. I felt good to be on my own but at the same time I wanted to be with Mike. I hadn't seen him for a week and was excited at doing so soon.

I was euphoric as I arrived at the airport and when I saw Mike approaching another rush of excitement went through me. He looked so handsome and well. We kissed and hugged and he placed a rope of Thai flowers around my neck. I anticipated magic with my lover, friend and companion in the Far East but not the levels of ecstasy we shared. I felt no jet lag, I was on far too much of a natural high.

We were chauffeured to the exclusive Ambassador Hotel The whole experience was magical. The incense burning in the Temples and the heavily scented flowers with which Mike decorated our bed contributed to a fantastic cocktail of exotica and erotica, which we both felt. And although Mike had sensed the delight of Bangkok when he worked there many years ago he said he was almost seeing it for the first time, through my eyes.

His brother Robin and sister-in-law Donna were also at the hotel, sharing the suite with us, as Mike was really keen for them to meet me. We hit it off straight away. The suite overlooked the most beautiful garden in which I could see numerous lizards basking on the walls. Through the windows I could also see the fantastically romantic temples that seemed to be everywhere. The table in our room was laden with the colourful and unrecognisable fruits of Thailand. Everything was absolutely breath taking.

Mike took me to the famous Jim Thompson shop which had the most amazing selection of beautiful silks I had ever seen after which we went to one of his favourite restaurants, the "Two Vikings", with it's amazing thirties ambience and wonderful gourmet food. Even that wasn't the end of an amazing day. After leaving the restaurant we took a samova – a three wheeled open taxi with a small motorbike engine – to a bar in a small, busy back street Mike knew to listen to a singer called Tony, who had apparently sang there for years. A magical evening.

Bangkok itself was magical in many ways with its food, flowers, temples, smells, the golden Buddhas, the exotic fruits laid out in baskets on the pavements, the goldshops. The whole experience took my breath away. Particulary when it was enhanced by the wild lovemaking which Mike and I enjoyed. We certainly reached new heights of passion and fulfilment.

One evening seemed to sum up the enjoyment and character of the place and the people. We went to a local fish supermarket come restaurant where, on arrival, we were allocated a "helper". A girl took our "supermarket" trolley and as she wheeled it around we chose our food. Fish, salad, fruit, wine, vegetables. Whatever. When we finished she took the contents to the check out and paid while we waited, seated, in the warm evening air in a romantic atmosphere of candles, waterfalls and moonlight. The chosen food was then served, cooked to our specification. Splendid. The whole experience and the attention Mike gave me left me feeling very special and very spoiled

Just before our time in Thailand came to an end the four of us went to Patia Beach, north of Bangkok, a most beautiful part of the country. We stayed at the Siam Bayshore Hotel, a most lovely and luxurious hotel overlooking the Gulf of Siam.

It was here that two things happened that couldn't have been more opposite in their effect on me. One was amusing and seemed to sum up the fun and pleasure we had all enjoyed on the trip. The other shattered the magic of it all for me.

The fun bit concerned ice cream. We had spent a morning fishing from a yacht and then cooking and eating our catch for lunch. A relaxing day full of fun. Later we went for dinks and dinner in a fantastic hotel restaurant when Robin spied the ice cream selection. He couldn't resist it and chose some served in a coconut shell with chocolate sauce poured liberally over it. He liked it so much he ordered another helping. And then another. He must have eaten four or five orders before accepting defeat. The next day he said the experience continued when he went to bed because he spent the whole night dreaming of coconut ice cream !

The second experience forced me to see my relationship with Mike in a different light and put the whole thing into a serious focus and made me face an unexpected reality.

Whilst in the hotel one day Mike asked me to get some photographs he had in his bag. When I picked up the bag a half empty packet of condoms fell to the carpet. I stood there and stared at them aghast. I felt sick at the implications. He later told me that he had used them at a massage parlour in Bangkok. I knew the place as I had gone with him on one of his visits. I had hated it but Mike seemed to enjoy the experience.

But as I stood and stared at the condoms I felt the world had stopped. I yelled at Mike " Now you've fucked it all up. I'm leaving for Australia"

He yelled back as he threw a bottle of hand cream across the room " Please yourself"

"I will" I continued to yell "This isn't what I need or want"

Mike tried to tell me that it wasn't anything to do with our relationship and wasn't any reflection on how he felt about me. He said he still loved me. But I was shocked and deeply hurt. I was also worried about what else he was doing behind my back. I didn't want to catch anything because of his stupidity and was furious with him. At least I rationalised to myself that if I ever did catch something it would be as a result of my own indiscretions, not somebody else's. I wanted to leave him but I didn't.   But our relationship was damaged irreparably.

The stay came to an end all too soon and Robin and Donna returned home to San Francisco whilst Mike and I went on to Hong Kong.

.

TWENTY EIGHT

We were met at the airport by a chauffeur driven Rolls Royce and driven to the Hotel Peninsular.

Hong Kong was completely and fascinatingly different from anything else I had ever experienced anywhere in the world.

The ferry trip along the river from Kowloon to Aberdeen where we discovered the amazing and colourful floating restaurants. The river itself alive with junks, music and carnival activities. It was both eery and wonderful all at the same time. The restaurants were incredible, all patterned with colourful mosaics lining their walls and all full of baroque furniture. The restaurant in which we ate was on an old, very big boat and the food was delicious and quite different.

One evening we dined at the unique, old colonial Repulse Bay Hotel. Wall to wall waiters, decorative fans whirling above our heads to cool us as we sipped Singapore Slings. Out on to the Terrace which overlooked the most exotic looking and sweetest smelling gardens. Allied to a full moon in a star studded sky it was a truly romantic and memorable evening

In fact the whole trip itself was romantic and memorable and the charms of Hong Kong were a strong aphrodisiac! I was forcing myself to suppress any thought of Mikes infidelities, knowing that he hadn't made any repeat visits to the massage parlour, and our love making was very soon back on the agenda.

A trip to Red China was an amazing day out. We took a small, hot, overcrowded train from Kowloon into a country which was very crowded, with very little, if anything to offer in the way of consumer products. We finished up taking photographs of some very sweet children at a nursery school and buying a real Chinese painting for eight dollars, which we were always unsure as to which way up to hang.

If the train in the morning was overcrowded it was nothing to compare to the return journey. An experience I would not like to repeat but would like to forget. It began with an hour long wait in the intense heat on a "platform" which was so crowded we couldn't move. To make matters worse I was attacked by a lobster! The girl next to me had a bag in which was carrying live lobsters and one of them had taken a fancy – or a dislike – to my leg, which it manifested by nipping me. And because it was so crowded and I couldn't move away I had no possibility of escaping its attentions. Mike and I both found it revolting and scary at the same time.

The train finally arrived and it was immediately obvious that it wouldn't hold everybody hoping to board. Luckily it had stopped with an open window right in front of us so Mike had the presence of mind to climb through it – and then pull me in behind him. The one and a half hour journey was quite something. It smelled as if every evil smelling drain in China was located right by the train line as we progressed and the smell was absolutely appalling. It was also so hot, humid and crowded I knew exactly how a sardine in a tin which had been placed in a Turkish bath must have felt. A poor duck that one old man was carrying appeared to die from the heat and exhaustion right in front of my eyes. On more than one occasion I felt I would just have to climb back out of the window through which we had entered the train so keenly to save myself from the terrible experience. I didn't and eventually we arrived back. It had been a long and interesting day!

Back in the luxury of our room at the Peninsular Hotel, wrapped in bath robes and sipping cooling gin slings we both agreed that we were glad of the experience and we wouldn't have missed it for the world. Easily said now it was behind us. To celebrate our return to normality, and comfort, we raised our glasses to the lobster we were about to eat. A lobster done the kosher way.

All too soon our time in Hong Kong was over and we were to be parted for three weeks, at the end of which we would be meeting up again in Eilat. Mike was returning to the desert to work and I was off to visit Ashley and his wife in Australia. Mike gave me all his spare cash, we kissed and hugged, and parted tearfully.

I had six hours to spare before my flight so I wandered round the shops and bought myself a camera to record my trip.

I missed Mike but being in Australia was a chance to relax and unwind after all the exotica and adventure.

Like a good champagne but without the bubbles.

THE WAR IN LEBANON

ARIELA

Ariel ties bright ribbons to her chairs in an attempt at gaiety. A multitude of cakes and biscuits cover her table, more will soon be taken from her oven. She washes clothes. She cannot sit and do nothing. She cannot relax and has to be doing things all the time. She waits near the phone for the calls from her three sons. They are all fighting in the war to be free. One said "Nothing to fear Mum, the bomb was 50 metres away". He is eighteen. Another says " Don't worry, Mum, I'm on the front line but in a tank. They won't get me". He is twenty. The third, who is twenty two, tells her nothing. She waits. She cooks. She washes. She is alone with her fear. She plays Beethoven. She hopes and prays. She is a mother and her sons are her life. What would she do without them.

NAOMI

Naomi was born in Tel Aviv. The city with its hustle and bustle isn't for her. She wants a different and special way of life. In Israel it is easy to find such a thing. There are Kibbutzim with their community living. There are Moshavim with their collective living. And there is utopia south of Eilat named Ophira. This is where she wants to live. At eighteen she does her two years military training and works on a kibbutz. At the end of her service she can make a barren waste into a most exotic garden of beauty. She leaves the army and takes her few bits and pieces and hitches a ride to Ophira. She rents a beach hut. It is more than adequate for her simple needs and she feels it is very special. She loves the place. She can see Jordon to her left and the Straights of Terran on her right. In the middle , like

150

a sandwich, are the purple & pink mountains full of beauty and mysticism.

Gil is a diver and her neighbour. They become good friends and then lovers. They share Naomi's hut and lead a good and happy life. The town is small. Fifty families or so. The local restaurant/Bar always filled with familiar and dear friends. They are a self contained group, away from the world, but very much part of it. The town is hand built but is a bone of contention in the far east.

They have been in Ophira for four years when their paradise becomes a pawn in the peace process. Prime Minister Menachim Begin, of Israel and Anwar Sadat of Egypt sign a peace treaty. As a result Ophirs and all the south of Eilat is to be handed over to Egypt. The transfer is to take place in two years time. Everybody feels angry and betrayed. People have died and suffered so much for this little piece of the desert. To give it up what cost so much is treason. The people tend their gardens, build more homes. The people are special and feel sure they won't have to give up their little piece of heaven on earth. Where will they go?

Sadat is assassinated and the people think that the peace process will die with him. But his successor, Mobarak wants to continue the process and it carries on.

It is only two months before the time to leave and relinquish the land to Egypt. With heavy hearts Naomi and her friends search for another home. They look in the northern tip of the Sinia in a town called Eilat. They consider it a town for tourists and money. Not their sort of place. But they feel they have no choice. Although the government are paying compensation to help the move everybody feels thoroughly disheartened. Money cannot replace what they are losing. A way of life.

Six weeks to go and Naomi and Gil view a house in Eilat on the very edge of the desert. Not expecting to like it they are pleasantly surprised to find it "speaks" to them. It says "welcome". They raise the money and buy it.

Naomi, Gil and their friends watch in indescribable horror as the bulldozers crush everything to dust. Naomi has been crying for days in anticipation of this moment. The Israelis feel they have to raze the small settlement to the ground so the Egyptians can't use it as a strategic base.

Everybody is in a stupor as they pack their belongings in the truck and slowly, silently and heartbrokenly make their way to Eilat and a new future.

And hopefully to peace.

TWENTY NINE

My last few months in Eilat were very difficult. It had lost its charm, as had the Sinai. I sold the house and sold most of the contents in a garage sale and shipped what was left to England. The weather was getting hotter and hotter and my friends were mostly leaving for the north. Mike reminded me that we had less than a hundred days to pass before we left. I did not know how I could face them in Eilat which seemed to getting smaller and more claustrophobic. I spent a weekend at the airbase where Mike worked which was interesting. It was being run down in anticipation of a hand over to the Israelis. I hoped it would play a part in the peace.

Both Mike and I felt that we had had enough and the time seemed to drag. Mike had spent three years in the desert and I had had my four years out of the "real" world. The house was sold and we moved into a suite at the Centre hotel for the last few weeks. This seemed strangely "spooky" to me as this was the hotel I had actually stayed in when I first came out to Eilat all those years ago.

I passed the time as best I could and wrote a lot, particularly long letters, many of which never got posted. They were mostly cathartic.

Ben was working as the manager of a hotel in Jerusalem and he and Dina seemed to be getting along OK. I had said my "goodbyes" to them but we had agreed that we would keep in touch. Ben was very upset to think that I would be physically out of touch soon and continued to call me every few days.

I sat in the square to savour my last few days in Eilat. I realized that I had developed a love/hate

153

relationship with the place and that I had no regrets at leaving it for good.

The evening of our departure arrived and I looked, for the last time, at the pink mountains reflecting in the Red Sea. Mike slowly zipped his monogrammed velcro case together, raised his beautiful blue eyes towards me and poured two glasses of champagne. We toasted "The Life. L'Chaim". The cab honked impatiently. Mike walked to the cab with his glass of champagne in his hand and I followed along behind with tears in my eyes. But not in my heart. Mike took my hand and we kissed for the last time in Eilat.

"Goodbye Eilat. You gave us your best. Goodbye forever. On to the world and whatever it holds."

We had eaten our lobster in the most kosher way.

In Israel, on the very red and biblical sea.

LETTER TO A DEAD FRIEND

Dear Miles

It's ages since we had lunch together and I talked your head off with all my problems. No more rent collections, Ben sold it for me for £8,500. He got all the vampires out.

Miles, I wish you hadn't decided to die. That's a silly thing for me to say, but I often think of you and miss you and want to talk to you. I don't have so many problems these days, you will be pleased, and no doubt surprised, to hear. I bought a house in Eilat, but I have now sold it and am leaving Israel. Remember when I told you to come and stay in the sun but you wouldn't leave your mother. What good did it do? You're dead, your horrible brother and sister-in-law (what was her name?) have your nice home and your mother is popped out of the way in a nursing home.

Wonder how our old boss, Colin, is getting on. It all seems like a different world, another life. No more drug company, no more long company lunches, with the occasional two hours work when we thought we should get some sales. Remember? What do you do all day now, Colin. I remember you liked riding but perhaps you aren't in the horse section now. Your funeral was horrible. There was me and Colin, that foreign doctor you liked and Ernie – oh yes, and that nice women who worked at the hospital you called on – Yoshke, that's her name. The rest were dreary relatives that you had always tried to avoid.

They were all crying but I can hear you laughing with that "Huw Haw" that Martin does so well. Martin had one of his things on Tele the other day. Don't suppose you saw it. You didn't like TV too much did you? Mike does. He's a lovely man. You would like him, perhaps I'll introduce you one day. We'll have a party.

I've been to lots of wonderful places. Thailand, Hong Kong, China, Cyprus, the Canaries. Oh, and Australia. Ashley lives there now with his wife.

I haven't worked for ages. I sometimes take little trips into the desert to show tourists the sites. Allied Irish are getting above themselves at the moment, demanding I pay the overdraft. You know my views. I agree with Lady Asquith when she said "If you don't die with an overdraft, you haven't lived" Perhaps you've met her where you are, or are men and women separated up there

Well. Miles, see you not too soon I hope. You were silly to go so soon. You should have visited me in the sun. We could have worked out a lifestyle for you. You've probably got a different one now.

Oh, Simone had a baby, so did Nora, still not married to Tony. Sue is going mad and I'm in love.

And just to let you know because you never believed me that it was possible. I have eaten Kosher lobster in Israel. It was delicious. You would have loved it.

If you see my Aunty Janey, Ivan or Mrs Elsley, give them all my love.

Now, nowhere to send this letter.

Lots of love